D0850697

MEDICINE
AND THE LAW

THE ENCYCLOPEDIA OF
HEALTH

MEDICAL ISSUES

Dale C. Garell, M.D. · General Editor

MEDICINE AND THE LAW

Neil Grauer

Introduction by C. Everett Koop, M.D., Sc.D.

Surgeon General, U.S. Public Health Service

CHELSEA HOUSE PUBLISHERS
New York · Philadelphia

The goal of the ENCYCLOPEDIA OF HEALTH *is to provide general information in the ever-changing areas of physiology, psychology, and related medical issues. The titles in this series are not intended to take the place of the professional advice of a physician or other health-care professional.*

Chelsea House Publishers
EDITOR-IN-CHIEF Nancy Toff
EXECUTIVE EDITOR Remmel T. Nunn
MANAGING EDITOR Karyn Gullen Browne
COPY CHIEF Juliann Barbato
PICTURE EDITOR Adrian G. Allen
ART DIRECTOR Maria Epes
MANUFACTURING MANAGER Gerald Levine

The Encyclopedia of Health
SENIOR EDITOR Paula Edelson

Staff for MEDICINE AND THE LAW
DEPUTY COPY CHIEF Nicole Bowen
EDITORIAL ASSISTANT Navorn Johnson
PICTURE RESEARCHER Villette Harris
ASSISTANT ART DIRECTOR Loraine Machlin
SENIOR DESIGNER Marjorie Zaum
PRODUCTION COORDINATOR Joseph Romano

First Printing

1 3 5 7 9 8 6 4 2

Library of Congress Cataloging-in-Publication Data

Grauer, Neil.
  MEDICINE AND THE LAW / Neil Grauer; introduction by C. Everett Koop.
    p. cm. — (The Encyclopedia of health. Medical issues; 79)
  Bibliography: p.
  Includes index.
  Summary: Examines legal and ethical issues relating to medicine
and the law.
  ISBN 0-7910-0088-5
       0-7910-0526-7 (pbk.)
  1. Medical jurisprudence—Juvenile literature. [1. Medical
jurisprudence.]
I. Title. II. Title: Medicine and the Law.
III. Series.   89-10027
RA1051.G33   1990   CIP
614′.1—dc20   AC

CONTENTS

THE ENCYCLOPEDIA OF
HEALTH

PREVENTION AND EDUCATION: THE KEYS TO GOOD HEALTH

C. Everett Koop, M.D., Sc.D.
Surgeon General,
U.S. Public Health Service

The issue of health education has received particular attention in recent years because of the presence of AIDS in the news. But our response to this particular tragedy points up a number of broader issues that doctors, public health officials, educators, and the public face. In particular, it points up the necessity for sound health education for citizens of all ages.

Over the past 25 years this country has been able to bring about dramatic declines in the death rates for heart disease, stroke, accidents, and, for people under the age of 45, cancer. Today, Americans generally eat better and take better care of themselves than ever before. Thus, with the help of modern science and technology, they have a better chance of surviving serious—even catastrophic—illnesses. That's the good news.

But, like every phonograph record, there's a flip side, and one with special significance for young adults. According to a report issued in 1979 by Dr. Julius Richmond, my predecessor as Surgeon General, Americans aged 15 to 24 had a higher death rate in 1979 than they did 20 years earlier. The causes: violent death and injury, alcohol and drug abuse, unwanted pregnancies, and sexually transmitted diseases. Adolescents are particularly vulnerable, because they are beginning to explore their own sexuality and perhaps to experiment with drugs. The need for educating young people is critical, and the price of neglect is high.

Yet even for the population as a whole, our health is still far from what it could be. Why? A 1974 Canadian government report attributed all death and disease to four broad elements: inadequacies in the health-care system, behavioral factors or unhealthy life-styles, environmental hazards, and human biological factors.

To be sure, there are diseases that are still beyond the control of even our advanced medical knowledge and techniques. And despite yearnings that are as old as the human race itself, there is no "fountain of youth" to ward off aging and death. Still, there is a solution to many of the problems that undermine sound health. In a word, that solution is prevention. Prevention, which includes health promotion and education, saves lives, improves the quality of life, and, in the long run, saves money.

In the United States, organized public health activities and preventive medicine have a long history. Important milestones include the improvement of sanitary procedures and the development of pasteurized milk in the late 19th century, and the introduction in the mid-20th century of effective vaccines against polio, measles, German measles, mumps, and other once-rampant diseases. Internationally, organized public health efforts began on a wide-scale basis with the International Sanitary Conference of 1851, to which 12 nations sent representatives. The World Health Organization, founded in 1948, continues these efforts under the aegis of the United Nations, with particular emphasis on combatting communicable diseases and the training of health-care workers.

But despite these accomplishments, much remains to be done in the field of prevention. For too long, we have had a medical care system that is science- and technology-based, focused, essentially, on illness and mortality. It is now patently obvious that both the social and the economic costs of such a system are becoming insupportable.

Implementing prevention—and its corollaries, health education and promotion—is the job of several groups of people:

First, the medical and scientific professions need to continue basic scientific research, and here we are making considerable progress. But increased concern with prevention will also have a decided impact on how primary-care doctors practice medicine. With a shift to health-based rather than morbidity-based medicine, the role of the "new physician" will include a healthy dose of patient education.

Second, practitioners of the social and behavioral sciences—psychologists, economists, city planners—along with lawyers, business leaders, and government officials—must solve the practical and ethical dilemmas confronting us: poverty, crime, civil rights, literacy, education, employment, housing, sanitation, environmental protection, health care delivery systems, and so forth. All of these issues affect public health.

Third is the public at large. We'll consider that very important group in a moment.

Fourth, and the linchpin in this effort, is the public health profession—doctors, epidemiologists, teachers—who must harness the professional expertise of the first two groups and the common sense and cooperation of the third, the public. They must define the problems statistically and qualitatively and then help us set priorities for finding the solutions.

To a very large extent, improving those statistics is the responsibility of every individual. So let's consider more specifically what the role of the individual should be and why health education is so important to that role. First, and most obviously, individuals can protect themselves from illness and injury and thus minimize their need for professional medical care. They can eat a nutritious diet, get adequate exercise, avoid tobacco, alcohol, and drugs, and take prudent steps to avoid accidents. The proverbial "apple a day keeps the doctor away" is not so far from the truth, after all.

Second, individuals should actively participate in their own medical care. They should schedule regular medical and dental checkups. Should they develop an illness or injury, they should know when to treat themselves and when to seek professional help. To gain the maximum benefit from any medical treatment that they do require, individuals must become partners in that treatment. For instance, they should understand the effects and side effects of medications. I counsel young physicians that there is no such thing as too much information when talking with patients. But the corollary is the patient must know enough about the nuts and bolts of the healing process to understand what the doctor is telling him. That is at least partially the patient's responsibility.

Education is equally necessary for us to understand the ethical and public policy issues in health care today. Sometimes individuals will encounter these issues in making decisions about their own treatment or that of family members. Other citizens may encounter them as jurors in medical malpractice cases. But we all become involved, indirectly, when we elect our public officials, from school board members to the president. Should surrogate parenting be legal? To what extent is drug testing desirable, legal, or necessary? Should there be public funding for family planning, hospitals, various types of medical research, and medical care for the indigent? How should we allocate scant technological resources, such as kidney dialysis and organ transplants? What is the proper role of government in protecting the rights of patients?

What are the broad goals of public health in the United States today? In 1980, the Public Health Service issued a report aptly entitled *Promoting Health-Preventing Disease: Objectives for the Nation.* This report expressed its goals in terms of mortality and in terms of intermediate goals in education and health improvement. It identified 15 major concerns: controlling high blood pressure; improving family planning; improving pregnancy care and infant health; increasing the rate of immunization; controlling sexually transmitted diseases; controlling the presence of toxic agents and radiation in the environment; improving occupational safety and health; preventing accidents; promoting water fluoridation and dental health; controlling infectious diseases; decreasing smoking; decreasing alcohol and drug abuse; improving nutrition; promoting physical fitness and exercise; and controlling stress and violent behavior.

For healthy adolescents and young adults (ages 15 to 24), the specific goal was a 20% reduction in deaths, with a special focus on motor vehicle injuries and alcohol and drug abuse. For adults (ages 25 to 64), the aim was 25% fewer deaths, with a concentration on heart attacks, strokes, and cancers.

Smoking is perhaps the best example of how individual behavior can have a direct impact on health. Today cigarette smoking is recognized as the most important single preventable cause of death in our society. It is responsible for more cancers and more cancer deaths than any other known agent; is a prime risk factor for heart and blood vessel disease, chronic bronchitis, and emphysema; and is a frequent cause of complications in pregnancies and of babies born prematurely, underweight, or with potentially fatal respiratory and cardiovascular problems.

Since the release of the Surgeon General's first report on smoking in 1964, the proportion of adult smokers has declined substantially, from 43% in 1965 to 30.5% in 1985. Since 1965, 37 million people have quit smoking. Although there is still much work to be done if we are to become a "smoke-free society," it is heartening to note that public health and public education efforts—such as warnings on cigarette packages and bans on broadcast advertising—have already had significant effects.

In 1835, Alexis de Tocqueville, a French visitor to America, wrote, "In America the passion for physical well-being is general." Today, as then, health and fitness are front-page items. But with the greater scientific and technological resources now available to us, we are in a far stronger position to make good health care available to everyone. And with the greater technological threats to us as we approach the 21st century, the need to do so is more urgent than ever before. Comprehensive information about basic biology, preventive medicine, medical and surgical treatments, and related ethical and public policy issues can help you arm yourself with the knowledge you need to be healthy throughout your life.

FOREWORD

Dale C. Garell, M.D.

Advances in our understanding of health and disease during the 20th century have been truly remarkable. Indeed, it could be argued that modern health care is one of the greatest accomplishments in all of human history. In the early 1900s, improvements in sanitation, water treatment, and sewage disposal reduced death rates and increased longevity. Previously untreatable illnesses can now be managed with antibiotics, immunizations, and modern surgical techniques. Discoveries in the fields of immunology, genetic diagnosis, and organ transplantation are revolutionizing the prevention and treatment of disease. Modern medicine is even making inroads against cancer and heart disease, two of the leading causes of death in the United States.

Although there is much to be proud of, medicine continues to face enormous challenges. Science has vanquished diseases such as smallpox and polio, but new killers, most notably AIDS, confront us. Moreover, we now victimize ourselves with what some have called "diseases of choice," or those brought on by drug and alcohol abuse, bad eating habits, and mismanagement of the stresses and strains of contemporary life. The very technology that is doing so much to prolong life has brought with it previously unimaginable ethical dilemmas related to issues of death and dying. The rising cost of health-care is a matter of central concern to us all. And violence in the form of automobile accidents, homicide, and suicide remain the major killers of young adults.

In the past, most people were content to leave health care and medical treatment in the hands of professionals. But since the 1960s, the consumer of medical care—that is, the patient—has assumed an increasingly central role in the management of his or her own health. There has also been a new emphasis placed on prevention: People are recognizing that their own actions can help prevent many of the conditions that have caused death and disease in the past. This accounts for the growing commitment to good nutrition and regular exercise, for the fact that more and more people are choosing not to smoke, and for a new moderation in people's drinking habits.

People want to know more about themselves and their own health. They are curious about their body: its anatomy, physiology, and biochemistry. They want to keep up with rapidly evolving medical technologies and procedures. They are willing to educate themselves about common disorders and diseases so that they can be full partners in their own health-care.

The ENCYCLOPEDIA OF HEALTH is designed to provide the basic knowledge that readers will need if they are to take significant responsibility for their own health. It is also meant to serve as a frame of reference for further study and exploration. The ENCYCLOPEDIA is divided into five subsections: The Healthy Body; The Life Cycle; Medical Disorders & Their Treatment; Psychological Disorders & Their Treatment; and Medical Issues. For each topic covered by the ENCYCLOPEDIA, we present the essential facts about the relevant biology; the symptoms, diagnosis, and treatment of common diseases and disorders; and ways in which you can prevent or reduce the severity of health problems when that is possible. The ENCYCLOPEDIA also projects what may lie ahead in the way of future treatment or prevention strategies.

The broad range of topics and issues covered in the ENCYCLOPEDIA reflects the fact that human health encompasses physical, psychological, social, environmental, and spiritual well-being. Just as the mind and the body are inextricably linked, so, too, is the individual an integral part of the wider world that comprises his or her family, society, and environment. To discuss health in its broadest aspect it is necessary to explore the many ways in which it is connected to such fields as law, social science, public policy, economics, and even religion. And so, the ENCYCLOPEDIA is meant to be a bridge between science, medical technology, the world at large, and you. I hope that it will inspire you to pursue in greater depth particular areas of interest, and that you will take advantage of the suggestions for further reading and the lists of resources and organizations that can provide additional information.

MEDICINE AND THE LAW

The U.S. Supreme Court.

For more than a century (from its founding in the 1800s until the 1960s), the *Times* of London, the most distinguished newspaper in England, reserved its front page for news about the city's births, marriages, and deaths. Today, it seems odd that such commonplace events, which readers humorously dubbed "hatches, matches and dispatches," dominated the headlines. But the paper's publishers were not completely off base: Nothing, after all, is more essential to a city than the events that shape the daily life of its citizens.

The three milestones emphasized by the *Times* usually involve members of the medical profession. Today, in both England and the United States, a doctor and nurse are usually present when

13

people are born; in some areas a physician must approve one's health before he or she can get married and raise a family; and, in most cases, a doctor and other health-care workers are nearby when someone dies.

Health-care workers play an important role in human life and must answer to a high authority: the law. Indeed, every aspect of health care in the United States is governed by strict guidelines established by medical groups, regulatory agencies, federal and state legislatures, and the courts. The law requires, for example, that anyone who wishes to practice medicine must obtain a license. Certified practitioners whose efforts are sloppy or who harm their patients may be sued in court or face criminal prosecution and penalties. Federal and state regulations apply to organ transplants, new methods for helping couples to have babies, and research experiments that may lead to new medicines or medical knowledge. The courtroom has become a forum for heated debate about medical decisions that concern individuals, and there is much controversy about when someone can justly be pronounced dead.

The relationship between medicine and the law has become so complicated in recent years that medical schools now offer courses on health law. They cover abortion, consent by minors to medical treatment, death and dying, experimentation on humans, malpractice, mental-health law, and professional licensing.

Why has the practice of medicine become the focus of so many new laws and court cases? To some extent it is because health care itself has grown so dramatically, challenging ancient assumptions about birth and death, health and illness—and these assumptions often form the basis of legal statutes. In addition, courts now play a greater role than ever before in deciding matters of intense social concern: abortion, the rights of juveniles, and the rights of mental patients.

These developments are the result of the increasingly complicated questions surrounding the morals and ethics of medical practice. But throughout these changes one ancient medical principle, originally stated by the 5th-century B.C. Greek physician Hippocrates, stands unchanged. "Above all," he told his fellow doctors, "do no harm."

•   •   •   •

CHAPTER 1

A LEGAL HISTORY

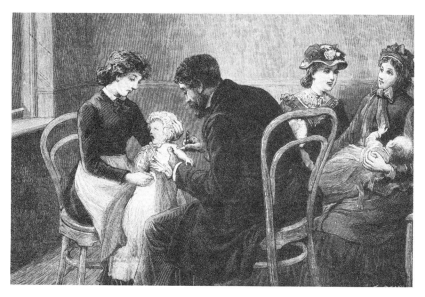

An engraving of a doctor inoculating a baby.

Some of the most controversial issues involving medicine and the law date back to antiquity. The issue of surrogate parenthood, for example, has a precedent in the Old Testament book of Genesis. When Sarah is unable to have a child, she instructs her husband, Abraham, to impregnate another woman, her handmaiden Hagar, who gives birth to Ishmael.

Laws governing who could practice medicine—and how it was to be practiced—also date back many centuries. Ancient doctors, like today's practitioners, were subject to penalties, which could be harsh. In the late 18th century B.C., Hammurabi, a king of ancient Babylon (what is now Iraq), imposed the Code of Hammurabi. It decreed, among other things, that if a physician operated on a badly wounded person who subsequently died or if he cost someone an eye in the course of operating on it, the doctor's fingers should be cut off. The code also regulated medical fees.

Perhaps the most universal medical law—and also one of the oldest—is imposed on doctors by themselves. It was created by Hippocrates, the ancient Greek who is often called the Father of Medicine. His oath is accepted by modern physicians, many of whom still take it when they become doctors. The key principles of the Hippocratic oath include the following: The welfare of the patient is a physician's top priority; the information a patient gives a doctor during the course of treatment must be kept confidential; medical privileges should never be abused; and doctors have a duty to pass on their knowledge to the next generation of healers. Hippocrates, however, cannot be blamed for a less admirable medical precedent established by the ancient Greeks: In about 300 B.C., they prohibited women from practicing medicine.

MEDICINE IN THE MIDDLE AGES

As long ago as A.D. 931, a board for examining and licensing healers was created in Baghdad, the capital of what is now Iraq. In 1140, Roger II, ruler of Sicily, the large island near the toe of Italy's boot, enacted a law that doled out punishment to anyone who practiced medicine without a license.

In 1225, Frederick II, ruler of the Holy Roman Empire (composed of what today are Germany and northern Italy), established a highly sophisticated medical-practice law. First, it required five years of schooling for would-be doctors. Next, they had to practice for one year under the supervision of an experienced physician. This qualified them to take an examination. If they passed it, they were given a license.

Frederick II's law did not end there. It also set standard fees for medical treatment, required doctors to administer care to the poor without charge, and prohibited them from owning drugstores. Lawbreakers could have their possessions confiscated and be sentenced to a year in prison.

Folk Healers

Impressive as these regulations were, they did not improve the medical care most people received. Only the upper classes could afford the services of university-educated physicians, and these physicians, for all their training, were not highly skilled.

The rest of the population relied on folk healers, which was not necessarily a disadvantage; folk healers often had more hands-on experience than did educated physicians. Many were women who had learned how to grow and prepare herbs that had true medicinal value. They also acted as midwives, helping other women give birth to and then care for their babies. These practitioners earned the name "wise women" from the poor people they treated. Some medical authorities, however, labeled them "witches" and banned their services.

Church and State

At this time, European universities came under the control of the Roman Catholic church, and religious leaders often restricted the legal practice of medicine to the graduates of specific schools. In 1229, for example, Pope Gregory IX granted medical licenses only to graduates of the university in Toulouse, France.

In the next centuries, the church shared power with secular governments in some countries, such as England. In 1422, the British Parliament passed a law requiring all physicians to have a university education, and in 1511, King Henry VIII founded the Royal College of Physicians and Surgeons, giving it and the archbishop of Canterbury the authority to grant licenses to doctors. In 1523, Parliament passed a law that allowed nonclergymen to practice medicine for the first time. Untrained doctors could practice medicine as long as they did not exaggerate their training or credentials.

THE NEW WORLD

In the 16th century, European nations established their first overseas colonies. Sometimes medical practice there came under laws established in the homeland. For example, Spanish colonies established in the early 1500s in Florida, California, and Latin America were covered by the Medical Code of Castile. (Castile was an ancient kingdom located in central Spain.)

Great Britain exercised less legal control over its colonies. It did not initially extend its medical regulations to its New World colonies, which were situated on the East Coast of North America. The settlers there had to protect themselves—and they did. In 1639, colonial Virginia passed a law requiring physicians to have a license. And in 1649, Massachusetts enacted a law regulating "chirurgeons [surgeons], midwives, Physitians [physicians] or others . . . employed at any time about the body of men, women or children, for preservation of life, or health" by requiring them to be licensed. In addition, no doctors could practice medicine "without the advice and consent of such as are skillful in the same Art (if such may be had) or at least some of the wisest and gravest then present." Violators could expect "such severe punishment as the nature of the fact may deserve."

New York passed a similar law in 1665. Its main objective was to regulate fees rather than to restrict licensing. The need for medical care was so great that anyone who showed some skill at it was generally allowed to practice.

Slow Gains and Regulation

As the colonies grew and developed, they looked to the example of Europe and its superior arts and sciences. Not that the Old World had come very far. Indeed, Voltaire, the 18th- century philosopher and wit, observed that medicine and the doctors who practiced it were good only for "amusing the patient while nature cures the disease." But American-trained doctors were even worse. In 1753, Dr. William Douglas of Boston, who had studied in England, maintained that patients tended by doctors taught in the New World faced "*more danger* from the Physician than from the Distemper [illness]."

Yet medical practice in the colonies made some gains. In 1765, the first North American medical school opened in Philadelphia, at what became the University of Pennsylvania. Its founder, Dr. John Morgan, lamented that many untrained physicians in America practiced "in a pitiful state of ignorance." Another observer noted that "quacks abound like locusts in Egypt . . . as the profession is under no kind of Regulation. Any man at his pleasure sets up for Physician, Apothecary [pharmacist], and Chirurgeon [surgeon]."

Skepticism was the order of the day. Thomas Jefferson was convinced that what doctors pretended to be legitimate treatment was, in fact, nothing more than keeping "alive the hope and spirits of the patient" with phony medications. "One of the most successful physicians I have ever known has assured me that he used more bread pills, drops of colored water, and powders of hickory ashes, than of all other medicines put together," Jefferson wrote to a friend. "It certainly was a pious fraud. . . . I believe we may safely affirm, that the inexperienced . . . band of [doctors] let loose upon the world, destroys more of human life in one year, than all the [criminals] do in a century."

Regulation, it seems, did not keep quacks from practicing. The laws regarding public health were much stricter, maintaining a tradition that the colonies inherited from England. In *Commentaries on the Laws of England*, published in 1769, legal scholar Sir William Blackstone wrote that "offenses . . . against the public health of the nation . . . [are] of the highest importance." The

A British caricature from the 1850s spoofs efforts to find the cause of cholera, which at that time was a national epidemic.

first crime addressed by Blackstone in his chapter on public health was the failure to obey an order of quarantine, which restricts the movement of persons afflicted with an infectious disease.

THE GOVERNMENT STEPS IN

When the U.S. Constitution was adopted in 1793, it made no mention of health laws or of the authority of the federal government to pass them. In part, this was because the individual states already had many local health laws that dealt with quarantine, food inspection, water, housing, and more.

For the next 100 years, the states continued to supervise public health, but the federal government stepped in during emergencies. One occurred in 1794, when Congress authorized President George Washington to change the site of its sessions after the outbreak of a contagious disease that contaminated their usual meeting place. In 1796, Congress acted again, this time giving the president the authority to help states enforce quarantines. In 1799, it widened his authority further, allowing him to help states quarantine ships arriving from foreign ports and to protect federal officials from contagious illnesses. Congress passed yet another health law in 1813; this one promoted the use of a cowpox vaccine by promising its free distribution to anyone who wanted it.

The National Board of Health

A major breakthrough in federal health policy occurred in 1878, when an epidemic of yellow fever claimed some 30,000 lives in the Mississippi Valley. This led Congress to create a National Board of Health and to fund it with $500,000. The board researched various means of containing the disease and was authorized to enforce a national quarantine system.

The board was abolished in 1884, a casualty of political infighting, but six years later the government reaffirmed its commitment to public health in response to an epidemic of cholera, a severe form of diarrhea caused by germs that attack the intestines. Anxious to limit the spread of the disease, Congress passed

A World Health Organization poster from 1980 announces that smallpox has effectively been wiped out. A 1905 Supreme Court case involving smallpox vaccinations determined that the government has the right to limit personal freedom in the interest of public health.

a federal quarantine law. The lawmakers cited the federal government's power to regulate interstate commerce, which could spread epidemics.

For the most part, the states remained in control of medicine. As the nation's population grew, however, individual communities wanted more control. The first state law authorizing local health boards was passed in Massachusetts in 1797. But the states did not use this authorization until 1866, when New York established the Metropolitan Board of Health, which was the first of the local health boards.

THE MODERN ERA

As the 20th century approached, medical science made large strides, as did public interest in upgrading health standards. States promoted public-education drives and opened clinics for the treatment of tuberculosis and venereal diseases. By 1909, every state in the Union had a board of health.

At the same time, the federal government got more involved in health and medical matters. In 1905, the U.S. Supreme Court ruled in the landmark case *Jacobson v. Massachusetts* that the government had the right to limit personal freedom in the interest of public health. At issue was the Board of Health of Cambridge, Massachusetts, which required people to be immunized against smallpox. The plaintiff, one Mr. Jacobson, feared that the smallpox vaccine might harm him; he claimed he had a right to refuse an injection and risk getting the disease. The Supreme Court disagreed and held that the board of health could force him to be vaccinated if it believed that would protect others from the spread of illness.

The government entered the health scene again in 1906, when it passed the Pure Food and Drug Act, the first law ever to establish standards for foods, drugs, medical devices, and cosmetics. In 1918, Congress passed the Venereal Disease Act, which provided federal funds to the states for health purposes.

Today, all 50 states have a compulsory-immunization law. Most require that children of a certain age be immunized against

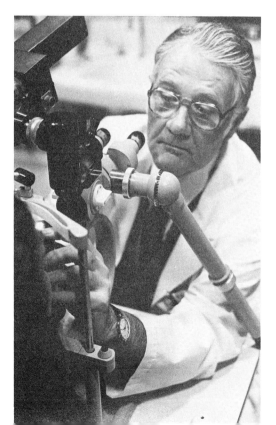

Twenty-six states require children to take annual vision and hearing tests.

polio, whooping cough, and diphtheria. (Some state immunization laws, however, make exceptions for children whose religious beliefs bar vaccinations.) Twenty-six states also require that children be given vision and hearing tests; 16 states require physical examinations for youngsters when they begin school; 10 require dental examinations; and 14 require schools to keep health records for schoolchildren.

The Feds Take Charge

In recent times, the federal government has employed several different tactics in its attempt to safeguard public health. For example, it has devised specific postal regulations to keep quack medicines and medical devices out of the mails. It has also used its military authority to establish comprehensive health-care programs for the armed services.

But the most effective weapon the government has wielded against medical fakes and frauds has been regulatory agencies, such as the Food and Drug Administration (FDA), which can override rulings at the state level on specific medicines. For example, in the late 1970s, several states legalized the use of laetrile, an apricot-pit derivative that some people claimed was helpful in treating cancer. But according to the FDA, laetrile's effectiveness had not been proven, and the agency outlawed its transportation from one state to another, thus overriding the state laws that had legalized the drug. The FDA took a less stringent view in 1988, when it allowed Americans suffering from acquired immune deficiency syndrome (AIDS) to bring small amounts of certain unapproved drugs into the United States for their personal use.

Federal Funding

The federal government does not only police public health; it also encourages breakthroughs. In 1950, the government invested $50 million in health care and research. By 1979, the amount had reached $50 billion. Vast sums were also poured into new facilities. In 1946, Congress passed the Hospital Survey and Construction Act, also known as the Hill-Burton Act. It funded the construction of private health-care facilities throughout the

LAETRILE WARNING

Cancer patients and their families are warned that

LAETRILE IS WORTHLESS

Whether sold as a drug (amygdalin) or as a "vitamin" (B-17), Laetrile is worthless in the prevention, treatment or cure of cancer. The substance has no therapeutic or nutritional value.

LAETRILE IS DANGEROUS

Laetrile can be fatal for cancer patients who delay or give up regular medical treatment and take Laetrile instead.

Laetrile contains cyanide and can cause poisoning and death when taken by mouth. One infant is known dead of cyanide poisoning after swallowing fewer than five Laetrile tablets. At least 16 other deaths have been documented from ingestion of Laetrile ingredients (apricot and similar fruit pits).

Laetrile is especially hazardous if the injection form is taken by mouth. This can cause sudden death.

LAETRILE MAY BE CONTAMINATED

Laetrile is not routinely subject to FDA inspection for quality and purity as are all other drugs.

Analysis has shown some Laetrile to contain toxic contaminants. Ampules of Laetrile for injection have been found with mold and other adulterants which can be dangerous when injected.

Those who persist in the use of Laetrile or its ingredients should:

• Be prepared to deal promptly with acute cyanide poisoning if the oral product is used. Vigorous medical treatment must be started immediately or death can result.

• Watch for early symptoms of chronic cyanide poisoning, including weakness in the arms and legs and disorders of the nervous system.

• Keep the drug out of reach of children.

GET THE FACTS

For full details about the hazards of Laetrile, see your family physician or a cancer specialist, or write the Food and Drug Administration, HFG-20, 5600 Fishers Lane, Rockville, Maryland 20857.

Donald Kennedy
Commissioner of Food and Drugs

A poster from the Food and Drug Administration warns about the dangers of laetrile, an apricot-pit derivative that some people believed could cure cancer. Studies by the National Cancer Institute have shown that laetrile does not limit cancer growths or extend cancer patients' lives.

country. In return, the new hospitals, clinics, and research centers were required to provide medical care to people who had been slighted in the past, such as the poor and ethnic minorities. Since it began, the Hill-Burton program has paid for more than 5,000 hospitals.

But a shadow darkened this grand project. For more than 30 years, some of the Hill-Burton Act's most important policies— free service, community service, and nondiscrimination—were not met, and many needy people went without health care. The problem was that the act did not give authorities the power to enforce certain parts of the statute. Not until 1979, in response to a lawsuit, did the federal Department of Health, Education and Welfare (HEW) establish comprehensive enforcement regulations.

Medicare and Medicaid

The most significant contributions the government makes to health care, at least in dollars, are the Medicare and Medicaid programs, both created in 1965. Medicare and Medicaid do not provide health services. Instead, they help pay the expenses of private and public practitioners for the health care they give to those unable to cover their own bills. Medicare assists the elderly and disabled; Medicaid helps the poor. They are enormous programs that account for 40% of all the money spent on health care in the United States.

Forty percent may seem like a lot. But in fact it is much less than the governments of most other industrialized countries pay. The British government, for example, lays out more than 85% of all the money spent there on health care. And its National Health Service (NHS) is less comprehensive than some others. Japan, Germany, Sweden, and France all spend equally vast sums.

These nations recognize that the cost of health care exceeds what most people can afford. For this reason, a number of political leaders in the United States, including two from Massachusetts—U.S. senator Ted Kennedy and Governor Michael Dukakis—favor a comprehensive health plan that would provide cost-free care for every citizen of the United States.

Senator Ted Kennedy of Massachusetts is one of a handful of political leaders who favor a comprehensive health plan that would provide cost-free care for every U.S. citizen.

Whether or not the United States ever creates a national health service, the government is destined to play a growing role in the issue of health care. Federal administrative agencies such as the FDA and the Department of Health and Human Services (HHS), whose combined annual budget exceeds that of almost every nation in the world, oversee large-scale health-care programs and see to the enforcement of laws involving issues such as drug treatment. Medicare and Medicaid pay medical bills for a large portion of the population. And the Supreme Court has made rulings—on abortion and other issues—that all the states must obey.

In fact, the government has become so powerful a force in health care that it must be careful not to run afoul of freedoms guaranteed to all citizens by the U.S. Constitution. For example, the government's power to conduct certain health inspections of employees of both federally and privately owned companies has been limited by court rulings citing the Fourth Amendment's ban on unreasonable government searches. And judges who have ruled on cases concerning the minimum level of health care provided to prisoners in jail have cited the Eighth Amendment's ban on cruel and unusual punishment. The partnership of medicine and the law, as the next chapter shows, is not always an easy one.

•   •   •   •

CHAPTER 2

· · · · · · · · · · · · · · ·

FERTILITY, INFERTILITY, AND ABORTION

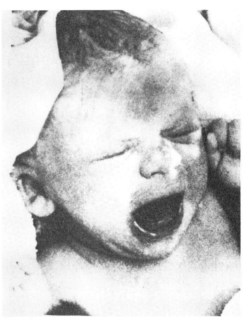

Louise Brown, the world's first test-tube baby.

The concern of medicine is life—helping to create it, preserving it whenever possible, easing its pains, making its ending as painless as possible. The first concern is birth, and since the beginning of history, lawmakers have placed it at the top of their agenda.

Because no society can survive without healthy new generations, some of the earliest-known laws have dealt with family planning and the issues it gives rise to: determining when a new life begins; whether it is permissible to prevent the conception of a child; when and whether it should be lawful to end a pregnancy by abortion.

BIRTH AND ABORTION THROUGH THE AGES

The oldest-known code of laws, King Hammurabi's, fined anyone who injured a pregnant woman in such a way that she could not give birth. Birth was so important in ancient Egypt that pregnant women who were found guilty of crimes were spared any physical punishment. It was against the law to obtain or cause an abortion. In ancient Greece, the Hippocratic oath included the vow that doctors would not "give to a woman an instrument to produce abortion."

A formidable dissenter from this policy was the 4th-century B.C. philosopher Aristotle. A proponent of population control, he urged doctors to perform abortions before the "animation of the fetus," that is, before a pregnant woman first sensed the movement of a developing baby in her womb, which Aristotle thought occurred 40 days after conception.

Ancient Rome also had laws concerning birth. In 600 B.C., its rulers required that the womb of every recently deceased pregnant woman be opened immediately so that the life of the child she was carrying might be spared. A legal code created in 449 B.C. decreed that human infants were born within 10 months of conception. This established a time period for determining whether a child was the legitimate offspring—and therefore the legal heir—of a man who had been absent or dead longer than that. More than 2,000 years later, the Code Napoléon, created by the French leader Napoléon Bonaparte in 1804, set the same time period between the conception and birth of a child and adopted the same legal principle.

Abortion Policies in the United States

Until the early 1800s, no scholarly books about medicine and the law had been written in the United States. The subject was not even taught in the nation's medical or law schools. The laws that dealt with medicine derived from the legal principles established by British statutes and from common law (the rulings of English judges).

This body of doctrine did not outlaw abortions performed prior to "quickening," or the first recognizable movement of the fetus inside a woman's womb. Even aborting a "quick fetus" was apparently not considered a crime. People in some states, however, felt differently. Connecticut passed a law banning abortion (the first one of its kind) in 1821; Illinois did the same six years later, and New York followed suit in 1828.

But the quick-fetus provision remained the basic rule until the Civil War, when more states enacted abortion laws. During the next decades, more and more people would consider the act of abortion a crime, and the penalties for it increased. By the end of the 1950s, most states had banned all abortions except those performed to save the life of the woman. This policy would remain until the ground-breaking *Roe v. Wade* case in 1973.

Contraceptives

At the same time that abortion laws developed, several states banned the sale or distribution of contraceptives—devices designed to prevent a woman from conceiving a child. In the 19th century, selling such items was outlawed under the same provisions that banned producing or distributing obscene materials. It was often illegal even to provide information about contraceptives. In 1873, Congress passed a federal statute known as the Comstock Law, named after Anthony Comstock, a crusader against what he considered pornography. The law banned the mailing of "obscene or crime-inciting matter" and included in its broad definition of such material "every article, instrument, substance, medicine, or thing . . . calculated to lead . . . [a person] to use or apply it for preventing conception or producing abortion." This law was amended in 1971. The provision about contraceptives was dropped, but not its prohibition against mailing anything that could produce an abortion.

THE SUPREME COURT RULES

The issue of "domestic relations" is not one on which federal courts have traditionally ruled. But they did become involved in the 1960s, when a debate arose over the extent to which a state could curb individual freedoms guaranteed by the U.S. Constitution. In 1965, the Supreme Court ruled (*Griswold v. Connecticut*) that a Connecticut law banning the use of contraceptives by a married couple was unconstitutional. "Would we allow the police to search . . . marital bedrooms for telltale signs of the use of contraceptives?" wrote Justice William O. Douglas, expressing the majority opinion of the court. "The very idea is repulsive to the notions of privacy surrounding the marriage relationship."

In 1972, the Court expanded its concept of the right of privacy beyond "the marital bedroom." It ruled that "if the right of privacy means anything, it is the right of the *individual*, married or single, to be free from unwarranted governmental intrusion into matters so fundamentally affecting a person as the decision whether to bear or beget a child." Soon after, the Court held (*Eisenstadt v. Baird*) that these privacy rights also applied to teenagers, when it overturned a New York law that banned the sale or distribution of contraceptives to persons under the age of 16.

Roe v. Wade

In 1973, the Supreme Court issued one of its most controversial rulings, holding in *Roe v. Wade* that the right of personal privacy included the "fundamental" but "qualified" right of a pregnant woman to have an abortion when she has consulted with a physician. The key concept was the "viability" of the fetus, which the Court defined as the point at which the fetus is "potentially able to live outside the . . . womb . . . with artificial aid." It was only after viability had been reached that the state had a "compelling interest" in the life or health of the fetus and could attempt to influence a woman's decision on whether to have an abortion.

Most fetuses reach the point of viability after the first six months—the second "trimester"—of a normal nine-month pregnancy. The Supreme Court recognized, though, that because the point of viability "may differ with each pregnancy," neither the state legislatures nor the courts could pinpoint a single factor that determines when viability is reached in each and every pregnancy. That decision rests with the attending physician in each case.

In 1986, a Massachusetts law that sought to give parents the power to stop a "competent" or "mature" teenager from having

Norma McCorvey, the plaintiff in Roe v. Wade, *at a political rally.*

an abortion was also judged unconstitutional by the Supreme Court. It ruled that a teenager who is "sufficiently mature to understand the [abortion] procedure and to make an intelligent assessment of her circumstances with the advice of her physician" has the right to obtain a abortion. But the Court qualified that opinion, stating that its ruling did not mean "that every minor, regardless of age or maturity, may give effective consent for the termination of her pregnancy." The Court added that an alternative to parental consent might be for the teenager to prove her maturity and competence by seeking permission for an abortion from a judge, an administrative agency, or some other authority, which would keep the matter confidential.

Several states have passed laws that restrict the access of teenagers to abortions, and court rulings on these laws indicate that some limits on the right to an abortion may be constitutional. For example, in 1988, a federal court in Minnesota (*American*

Liberties Union v. Minnesota) upheld a state law there that requires women under the age of 18 to notify both parents or get special approval from a judge before having an abortion.

The abortion issue does not affect only women. The Supreme Court also has wrestled with the question of whether the man who fathered the fetus is entitled to be told of the woman's plans to have an abortion and whether he has the right to stop it. The Court has decided that the woman's constitutional right to have an abortion during the first 6 months of her pregnancy cannot be denied by the father. Federal courts in Rhode Island and Kentucky (*Planned Parenthood v. Danforth*) have ruled that laws in those states requiring advance notice to the father of an intended abortion also are unconstitutional.

Related Issues

Since *Roe v. Wade*, the Supreme Court has ruled on a wide variety of issues relating to abortion. For example, it has found that a state may require doctors or health-care facilities to keep records regarding the abortions they perform and report periodically to the state about them; that states are not required to pay for abortions performed on Medicaid patients; that a state, city, or town may not adopt zoning or licensing laws meant to keep an abortion clinic from opening; that a state cannot outlaw abortion services from advertising; and that a health-care provider cannot be forced to perform an abortion if he or she is opposed to the procedure.

The changes in the laws regarding abortions have been more dramatic, widespread, and controversial than in any other area of medicine. According to *Law for the Medical Office*, published in 1984 by the American Association of Medical Assistants, since the Supreme Court first ruled in 1973 that state criminal laws banning abortions were unconstitutional, abortion has become the most common surgical procedure in the United States, ending one out of every three pregnancies.

The controversy over abortion undoubtedly will continue as some states persist in their efforts to limit the procedure and others seek to make it more available. Those who are religiously or philosophically opposed to abortion also have urged adoption of a constitutional amendment banning abortions, and the debate over that continues as well.

THE LAW AND FERTILITY

The courts have also ruled in cases involving people who want to have children. Judges have tackled the complex issues surrounding forced sterilization (in which persons are required to undergo medical procedures that render them unable to have children); test-tube babies; surrogate mothers; and deformed and handicapped children.

Forced Sterilization

In 1927, the Supreme Court upheld (*Buck v. Bell*) a state law that permitted mentally retarded people to be sterilized without their consent. The case involved a retarded 17-year-old girl— herself the child of a mentally retarded woman—after the teenager had already given birth to an illegitimate child. "Society can prevent those who are manifestly unfit from continuing their kind," wrote Justice Oliver Wendell Holmes, Jr.

The Court later modified its overall view of forced sterilization. For example, it overturned (*Oklahoma v. Skinner*) an Oklahoma law that permitted the sterilization of "habitual" criminals, ruling that the notion of "habitual" crime was ambiguous and ill defined. However, it has never reversed its 1927 judgment. States retain the authority to sterilize people judged "unfit" to have children, provided the procedure for determining the fitness is applied fairly.

Most cases dealing with forced sterilization involve a request by parents who want to ensure that their retarded but sexually active child does not become pregnant. These involuntary sterilizations are seldom controversial; it is generally assumed that parents act in the best interests of their children. But because the stakes are so high, doctors often ask a court to approve such a request before they perform the irreversible sterilization procedure.

In recent years, some criminal court judges have either recommended the forced sterilization of rapists or sought to compel

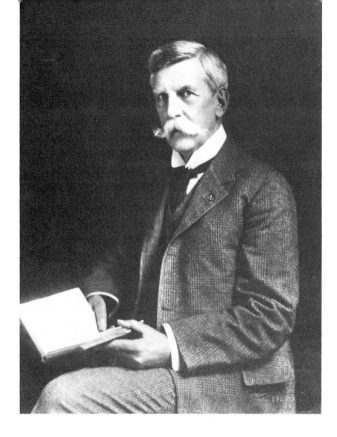

Supreme Court justice Oliver Wendell Holmes wrote the opinion in a 1927 case upholding a state law that allowed the sterilization of mentally retarded people without their consent. The Court later modified its stand on forced sterilization.

the sterilization of convicted child abusers—some of them women—by offering to reduce their prison sentences if they agree to be sterilized. For example, in 1988, a judge in Indiana told a woman who faced a possible 20 years behind bars for poisoning her 4-year-old son that he would reduce the sentence if she agreed to be sterilized. An Arizona judge sentenced a woman to take birth control pills for the rest of her childbearing years because she was convicted of leaving two infant sons alone in an apartment for three days. And judges in California, Texas, and Michigan, citing recent medical advances that permit the drug-induced, reversible sterilization of men, have proposed such a procedure as an alternative to regular penalties for sex offenders.

TEST-TUBE BABIES

Ever since the birth in 1978 of Louise Brown, the world's first test-tube baby (born, in England, as a result of a procedure in which her mother's egg and her father's sperm were first combined in a laboratory dish and then implanted in her mother's womb), the medical and legal professions have been tangled in a web of sticky issues. The controversies were summed up in a 1988 *Washington Post* headline that asked, "Whose Baby Is It, Anyway?"

Infertility—the physical inability of either a man or a woman to reproduce—is a widespread occurrence. It is estimated that of the 55 million American women of childbearing age (15–44), 1 in 10 has difficulty becoming pregnant. Since the late 1960s, however, medical technology has devised many solutions to the problem, and many couples want to employ them. According to a 1986 study by the American Medical Association (AMA), each year 1 million couples seek medical advice or treatment for infertility.

New Solutions to an Old Problem

Adoption used to be the favored option for childless couples. They applied to an agency that matched them with a child conceived by another couple and then signed legal papers accepting responsibility for the child. But medical technology has devised several different ways for infertile couples to have a baby, and most give the couple some genetic link to the child. All these medical procedures have raised serious legal issues that lawmakers and the courts have only begun to address.

The Donor Sperm Procedure This method is used by couples when the man is infertile. They obtain sperm placed in a sperm bank by an anonymous donor. The woman is then impregnated through artificial insemination. The resulting child is genetically linked to the mother (since it was her egg that the donor's sperm fertilized) but not to its legal father. The sperm donor, who is the child's biological father, has no legal connection to the child.

Surrogate Mothers These women substitute for females who are either infertile or at risk medically if they become pregnant. In these cases, the couples may find a surrogate mother, who is artificially inseminated with the man's sperm. She agrees to relinquish the resulting child after he or she is born, usually in return for a specific sum of money. The child is genetically linked to the father and to the surrogate mother but becomes the legal offspring of the couple. The donor sperm procedure and the use of a surrogate mother, both of which are illegal in some states, involve artificially inseminating the egg within the mother's womb. The following procedures are known as *in vitro* fertilization (IVF), which involves fertilizing an egg in a laboratory dish and then implanting it in a woman's womb:

- Test-tube babies: They are the offspring of couples who can produce sperm and eggs but for some reason fail to conceive a child. The couple's sperm and eggs are combined in a laboratory dish, and at least one of the fertilized eggs, or "preembryos," is implanted in the woman. The remaining preembryos may be frozen for possible use later. If the woman produces no eggs but is physically able to bear a child, an egg may be obtained from another woman, fertilized by the man's sperm, and then implanted in the first woman, who has the baby. The child is linked genetically to the father and the egg donor but is legally the offspring of the couple.

- Preembryos: These are created by another IVF procedure, in which a frozen, fertilized egg is obtained from another couple and implanted in the woman who wants to have a child. The baby is not genetically linked to either of its legal parents.

- Host uterus: In yet another IVF procedure, a couple may produce both sperm and eggs but the woman may be unable physically to bear a child. The couple's sperm and eggs are combined in a laboratory, and several of the resulting fertilized preembryos are implanted in a second woman, who has agreed to bear the child or children for the couple. The resulting offspring are genetically linked only to the couple.

None of these new IVF procedures is foolproof, but together they have produced an estimated 4,600 babies worldwide since the late 1970s. However, no regulations control the activities of the clinics that use the procedures, although some 25 states do have laws regarding artificial insemination, an older reproductive technique. And legislatures and the courts have far to go before they can sort out the complicated and sensitive legal issues surrounding IVF procedures.

Baby M

One highly publicized lawsuit was the Baby M case, which involved Mary Beth Whitehead, a surrogate mother who signed a contract with William and Elizabeth Stern that provided her $10,000 in return for allowing herself to be impregnated with Stern's sperm and then giving the Sterns the child she bore. When the baby was born, Whitehead changed her mind. She wanted to keep the child—a girl whose identity was protected in court papers by the name Baby M—and sought to have her contract with the Sterns invalidated.

In 1987, the New Jersey Supreme Court ruled that the surrogacy contract could not be enforced, but the judge also recognized that William Stern and Mary Beth Whitehead each had a legitimate claim to the infant. The court awarded custody of the baby to the Sterns but granted Whitehead the right to visit the child.

Unusual Cases

The Baby M case prompted a number of states to pass laws making surrogate mother contracts unenforceable. In 1988, Michigan became the first state to pass a law making it a crime

William and Elizabeth Stern after winning custody of Baby M in 1987. The Baby M case, which involved a baby who was born to William Stern and Mary Beth Whitehead under a surrogacy contract, prompted a few states to pass laws making such arrangements unenforceable.

to pay a surrogate mother anything other than medical expenses for her services.

The Australian state of Victoria had already made for-profit surrogacy illegal in 1984, when it passed the first comprehensive law dealing with new reproductive techniques. The law also bans the sale of human reproductive material, such as sperm. The next year, England banned commercialized surrogacy agreements, making it illegal for any person or company to act as a go-between in surrogacy agreements.

The new reproductive techniques have raised heated legal debate even in countries that have met the issues head-on. For example, in 1981, a wealthy American couple, Mario and Elsa Rios, used IVF procedures to create three preembryos with their donated sperm and eggs. One of the preembryos was implanted in Mrs. Rios, but she had a miscarriage. The couple, distressed by the failure of the IVF procedure, postponed a second try at having a baby and kept the remaining two preembryos frozen in storage in Australia.

In 1983, the Rioses died in an airplane crash, and a question arose: What should be done with the remaining two preembryos? A national legislative committee in Australia proposed that they be removed from storage and allowed to expire, but the parliament in the state of Victoria, where the preembryos were stored, rejected that recommendation. Instead, it passed a law requiring that an attempt be made to have the preembryos implanted in a surrogate mother. If and when the babies were born, they were to be put up for adoption.

It was presumed that the children would become the lawful offspring of the adopting parents, but it was not clear whether the babies would be entitled to inherit any of the Rioses substantial estate. In 1985, a court in the United States ruled that any children resulting from the Rios preembryos would not be the Rioses' heirs. Late in 1987, it was learned that the Rios preembryos were offered to another childless couple. It is not known whether they were implanted in the would-be mother or if a pregnancy resulted.

The debate over the Rios preembryos was by no means unique. When physicians use the IVF procedures to try to fertilize a woman's eggs with a man's sperm, often more than one egg is fertilized. Similarly, often more than one fertilized egg is implanted in the woman who wishes to become a mother, because it is unlikely that each egg will develop into a fetus. A problem then arises over what to do with the extra fertilized eggs or what to do if the fertility treatments lead to the development of three or four or five—or more—fetuses in a woman's womb, as sometimes happens.

Some people contend that unused or unwanted preembryos should be donated to other infertile couples who want to have a baby; others urge that the preembryos be used for research. As of 1989, such research was forbidden in the United States, but 6 other nations support the concept of research on preembryos up to the 14th day after their conception. Great Britain and Canada even allow the deliberate creation of preembryos for research purposes.

When fertility treatments result in a pregnancy involving multiple fetuses, some have to be aborted in order to give the remaining ones a better chance at normal development. In one case, a California couple sued their doctor because the fertility treatment the woman received resulted in septuplets—seven babies. Only three survived their birth. All have problems seeing, hearing, and breathing, and two suffer from cerebral palsy, a nerve disorder.

THE LAW AND GENETICS

Just as the law is either inadequate or silent on new reproductive technologies, so it has been unable to respond to issues raised by another area that has seen rapid advances: the study of genetic, or inherited, disorders. A U.S. Public Health Service Consensus Development Conference reported in 1979 that 3% to 5% of all new babies in the United States are born with birth defects, many of which are the result of genetic traits (as opposed to environmental factors such as drug use or poor nutrition).

In fact, birth defects cause 20% of the infant deaths in the United States. They are also the second leading cause of death in 1 to 4 year olds and the third leading cause of death for 15 to 19 year olds. Between 25% and 30% of all people under 18 years of age who are hospitalized in acute-care facilities go there for the treatment of genetic defects.

In the 1960s, concern about serious health problems led states to pass laws that called for the routine screening of newborn babies for genetic disorders that could be treated immediately. A 1985 study by the American Bar Foundation reported that 46 states and the District of Columbia had laws requiring genetic screening.

Doctors can now test potential parents for genetic problems and counsel them on the likelihood that their offspring will have genetic defects. They can also test fetuses to determine if they will be born with certain genetic problems, such as some kinds of mental retardation. This probing has become so commonplace that parents who are convinced that they did not receive proper counseling have sued their doctors and sought compensation for their emotional injury as well as for the illnesses suffered by their children.

Most courts have found that the parents of a disabled child are entitled to sue a physician for negligence. This is called a "wrongful birth" suit. But a much more difficult legal and moral question is raised by "wrongful life" lawsuits, in which a lawyer representing the parents and their child argues that the baby's condition is so bad that the youngster would be better off if he or she had never been born and that the doctor's negligence resulted in the baby's being alive.

Cases of this type have been rejected by most courts, and the few that have accepted them have been reluctant to accept the idea that a child suffering from a congenital disease or defect would be better off dead. Some courts have granted compensation to children for the monetary losses they have incurred or may incur in the future as a result of their congenital illness or defect. However, general damages for pain and suffering have not been awarded.

All the recent advances in reproductive technologies have raised highly difficult questions. As the 20th-century English philosopher C. S. Lewis wrote, "Each new power won by man is a power over man as well." Perhaps doctors and scientists have become the legal captives of their own creativity.

•   •   •   •

CHAPTER 3

WHODUNIT?

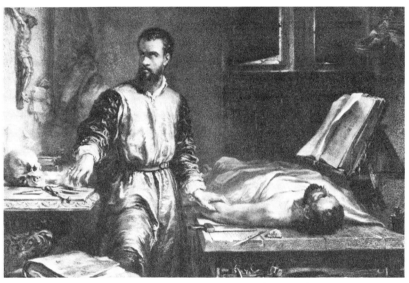

A woodcut of the 16th-century anatomist Vesalius performing an autopsy.

'' 'You are aware that no two thumb-marks are alike?','' (asked Inspector Lestrade).
'' 'I have heard something of the kind','' (replied Sherlock Holmes).

—Sir Arthur Conan Doyle,
The Adventure of the Norwood Builder

Since the earliest recorded times, medical knowledge—or what was thought to be medical knowledge—has been used to resolve legal issues. The first-known law codes and the most ancient religious texts included medical information that was supposed to help determine the answers to questions of life and death, innocence and guilt.

Chapter 2 mentioned birth and abortion. This chapter will trace other issues that involve both medicine and the law: whether a person died naturally or was murdered; what caused a person's death; what should be done to protect the public from the spread of disease; whether someone is rational, mentally defective, or insane; and how physicians should practice medicine.

This last issue, like so many others, can be traced back to the beginning of recorded history. Sections of the laws of ancient Egypt, for example, specified how a physician should treat a patient, requiring doctors to follow the established practices of earlier physicians. These early Egyptian laws also provided detailed regulations about sanitation, such as how houses should be kept clean, what foods people could eat, and how the dead were to be disposed of. In ancient Persia (what is now Iran), the law penalized medical malpractice and severely punished those who sought and performed abortions.

FORENSIC MEDICINE

Under Emperor Justinian (A.D. 483–565), the law of ancient Rome recognized "forensic" medicine—the application of medical facts in court cases—and that the evidence given by doctors in a legal proceeding was special. "Physicians are not ordinary witnesses," the law stated. They "give judgment rather than testimony." This means that doctors have special knowledge about physical matters and qualify as "experts" who give opinions based on their medical learning. The Justinian laws also covered such subjects as how pregnancy could be proved, rape, poisoning, and mental illness.

In about 1100, a code of laws was established in Jerusalem that required a doctor to examine the body of a murder victim and report on what injuries were discovered and how they were caused. A century later, in 1209, Pope Innocent III said that courts should continue what was apparently the customary practice of appointing doctors to determine the nature of wounds.

A marble relief of the Roman emperor Justinian. During his reign, Roman law recognized that doctors with knowledge of forensic medicine could qualify as experts during court cases.

What prompted the pope to decide this was the case of a thief who was caught stealing in a church and then set upon by several persons, including a priest, who all stabbed him. The particular question was whether the priest had delivered the fatal blow.

In 1278, King Philip the Bold of France decreed that doctors should be called upon to use their expertise in legal matters involving medical questions. At about the same time, but a hemisphere away, Chinese law decreed that legal inquests (investigations) were required in cases when the cause of a person's death was questionable. *Hsi Yuan Lu* (Instructions to Coroners), a five-volume text published in about 1250, included information on a wide array of legal and medical issues: abortion, infanticide (the murder of infants), means for determining death, suicide, strangling, poisoning, and medical examinations of the dead. *Hsi Yuan Lu*, the most advanced book of its kind in existence, was continually revised and reissued for six centuries.

Europe made a giant stride forward in 1532 when *Constituio Criminalis Carolina*, a legal code named after Emperor Charles V, was published in Germany. It covered medical evidence of murder, suicide, pregnancy, poisoning, malpractice, the severity of wounds, and also the examination of accused persons to determine if they were insane. More important, the code required courts to call for medical evidence in certain cases and permitted the performance of autopsies (the opening and thorough examination of a dead body) to determine the cause of a person's death. This code "opened the way for legal medicine to develop as a separate discipline," according to historian R. B. H. Gradwohl, author of *Gradwohl's Legal Medicine*, published in 1976.

In 1666, Paulus Zacchias completed his monumental *Quaestiones medico legales* (Medicolegal questions), which dealt not only with medical laws but also with public-health issues. It was the most thorough book of its kind written in Europe for many years. By contrast, the first major book in English on medicine and the law, published in 1788, was a slim 139-page text that staggered under the fat title *Elements of Medical Jurisprudence; or a succinct and compendious description of such tokens in the human body as are requisite to determine the judgment of a coroner and courts of law, in cases of divorce, rape, murder, etc. To which are added directions for preserving the public health.*

Among the customs of English law brought to North America by settlers in the early 1600s was the coroner's inquest, a legal proceeding that involves a hearing aimed at determining the cause of a person's death. The first record of a colonial inquest is from the winter of 1635, in Plymouth, Massachusetts. It involved the death of a man named John Deacon. The inquest report says: "Having searched the dead body, we find not any blows or wounds, or any other bodily hurt. We find that bodily weakness caused by long fasting and weariness, by going to and from, with the extreme cold of the season were the causes of his death."

The Scientific Method

It would be several hundred years, however, before the first scientific methods were developed for detecting not only how a person died but also, in the case of murder, who might be guilty of the crime. Analyzing fingerprints, for example, originated during the 1890s, when British law-enforcement officials in India, then an English colony, used these unique markings to identify suspected criminals. Great Britain's police force did not adopt the system of fingerprinting criminals until 1901; this tardiness amused the fictional private eye Sherlock Holmes, who commented on it sarcastically in the classic tales written by Sir Arthur Conan Doyle.

Fingerprints are generally allowed as evidence by American courts. More controversial is the use of voiceprints—graphic analyses of the intensity, timing, and frequency band of a person's speech—to identify a suspect. Also questionable is the reliability of the polygraph, or lie-detector test, which is believed by most of the scientific community to lack accuracy. Indeed, some judges have found mention of these tests during a trial so damaging to the fairness of a case that they have declared a mistrial, halted the proceedings, and demanded that a new jury be picked so the whole case can start over again.

High-tech Evidence

Nevertheless, as former *Baltimore Sun* journalist J. S. Bainbridge, Jr., said, "the march of science into the country's criminal courtrooms will continue." Bainbridge, who specializes in covering legal cases, made that statement in a 1987 article about a Maryland appeals court's refusal to accept as evidence a new medical technique called chromosome variant analysis, or DNA fingerprinting.

This form of analysis is a scientific test that compares the strands of deoxyribonucleic acid (DNA), the basic building block of everyone's genes, found in human tissue or bodily fluids. All living matter contains DNA, and remnants of it can also be found in the tissue, bones, and blood of dead matter. DNA is a basic material in the chromosomes found in the nucleus of a cell. It is made up of smaller units called nitrogenous bases. The order in which these bases occur determines each person's genetic makeup. Except in the case of identical twins, however, each person's DNA is unique, although it has characteristics that can be traced to the DNA in the genes a person inherits from a parent.

Scientists involved in criminal investigations take a sample of a suspect's tissue or bodily fluids, break down the DNA, and compare the pattern of bases in the sample with other DNA combinations. If two DNA samples match, either they come from the same person or from his or her parent or child. Advocates of DNA fingerprinting claim it is the most foolproof method yet devised for identifying suspects who have left minute clues—a drop of blood, a few hairs, or some semen—at the scene of a crime. This technique can also confirm whether someone is indeed the parent of a child.

Although the Maryland appellate court ruled in 1987 that chromosome variant analysis had not yet "shown to be generally accepted as reliable" by scientists, courts in 11 other states— New York, Virginia, Florida, North Carolina, South Carolina, Kentucky, Indiana, Ohio, Kansas, Oklahoma, and Idaho—have allowed DNA tests to be presented as evidence in trials.

History was made in July 1988 when genetic evidence led to the death penalty. It happened in Virginia, where a 26-year-old man was convicted of rape and murder based on the results of a DNA test performed on a sample of semen found on the victim's nightgown and on a nearby sleeping bag. The test revealed that the DNA taken from the crime scene matched DNA taken from a sample of the defendant's blood.

Even in Maryland, where the appellate courts would not accept DNA fingerprinting, a trial judge agreed to allow a sample of DNA to be taken from the bone marrow and teeth of a dead millionaire, buried for two years, in order to determine whether he had fathered a child born three months after his own death. A forensic doctor who testified for the state told the court that identifiable "DNA has been obtained from mummified bodies who have been dead for centuries. It was "highly probable," he added, that useful DNA samples could be obtained from the exhumed body of the millionaire and compared to samples taken from the infant. If they matched, the baby would be a lawful heir to his estate.

Clues to the Mind

As a rule, law courts accept forensic evidence only if it is demonstrably precise, as old-fashioned fingerprinting has proved to be. But precision is never possible in one significant area of forensic medicine: psychiatry. Physicians trained in this discipline study the functioning of the human mind. Because the mind is so complex that it resists precise analysis, it may never be possible to determine whether a suspect knew what he or she was doing, whether it was wrong, or whether he or she was in control of his or her actions.

Thus, a psychiatrist can only offer an opinion, albeit an opinion based on years of medical training and experience. Courts treat this evidence gingerly because nothing triggers public outrage more than a successful plea of insanity. In fact, only a few criminal cases each year result in a verdict of not guilty by reason of insanity. But whenever it happens, the public—and even lawyers, judges, and doctors—worry that a defendant has "gotten away with murder."

Early Precedents

The debate over a criminal's responsibility for his or her criminal actions is as old as the Talmud, an ancient commentary on the Bible that warns it is an "ill thing to knock against an imbecile." And the controversy rages on, as many psychiatrists readily admit. Dr. Jonas Rappeport, medical adviser to the Baltimore City Circuit Court with nearly 40 years of experience in forensic psychiatry, observed in the January 1980 issue of *Baltimore* magazine: "We don't know what [legal] insanity is. That's a legal decision for a judge or a jury to determine. . . . At best, we give an educated guess on how a defendant was at a certain time. We would expect . . . to disagree with other psychiatrists. We don't have any meter" for measuring mental stability.

The test for insanity is not based on whether a defendant has a particular medical condition, but on whether he or she was capable of understanding and obeying the law when the crime was committed. The question of whether the defendant committed the crime usually is not in dispute: Everyone knows who did it. The issue is how his or her mind was operating at the time.

The ancient Greeks thought insane people could not be held responsible for their acts, a view adopted by the Romans and the early Christians. In England, however, the common law held that persons without full possession of their powers of reason could be found guilty of crimes they committed. The king, however, could pardon anyone he thought was not morally responsible for a crime because of insanity.

The English law, and the American law based on it, changed in 1843 when the 14 judges of the High Court in Britain's House of Lords ruled that Scotsman Daniel MacNaghten, a former mechanic, was hopelessly deranged. A jury then found him "not guilty on the ground of insanity" for having shot and killed a man he mistook for the prime minister of England. (He was actually the prime minister's private secretary.)

The judges recommended that the jury find MacNaghten not guilty by reason of insanity because "to establish a defense on the ground of insanity, it must be proved that, at the time of committing the act, the . . . accused was laboring under such a defect of reason, from disease of mind, as to not know the nature and quality of the act he was doing; or, if he did know it, that he did not know he was doing wrong."

A New Standard

The MacNaghten (often spelled M'Naghten) Rule, subsequently adopted in the United States, became known as the "right-wrong" defense: Could, or did, the accused know right from wrong? In many states, it remains the standard by which insanity issues are still judged, even though many psychiatrists think it is outmoded. In the mid-1960s, the American Law Institute (ALI), a group of lawyers that drafts model statutes for state legislature, proposed that a different standard for judging a person's sanity be adopted. In time, some 28 states replaced the MacNaghten Rule with one devised by the ALI. According to this rule, a defendant is found not guilty by reason of insanity if it is determined that at the time of the alleged crime, the accused, "as a result of mental disorder . . . lacks substantial capacity either to appreciate the criminality of his conduct or to conform his conduct to the requirements of the law."

The ALI standard retains portions of the old right-wrong test (it persists in the phrase "lacks substantial capacity to appreciate the criminality of his conduct"), but the new formulation adds a new twist. It is known as the "irresistible impulse" defense: The accused's mental disorder was so great that he simply could not "conform his conduct to the requirements of the law," even though he knew he was breaking it.

Second Thoughts

In recent years, the controversy over the role psychiatrists play in legal proceedings has intensified dramatically, mainly because the insanity defense has been used successfully in several celebrated cases.

One case involved the 1978 murder of San Francisco's mayor George Moscone and Harvey Milk, the city supervisor. The defendant, Dan White, a former city official and a onetime policeman, shot each man in his office and then surrendered to local police. The case instantly made headlines because Milk was gay, and White freely expressed his bias against homosexuals.

A psychiatrist hired by White's attorneys told the jury that White should not be held responsible for the crime; he compulsively ate junk food, and the sugar in it had aggravated a chemical imbalance in his brain, temporarily diminishing his mental capacity and control at the time he shot Moscone and Milk. This argument was dubbed the "Twinkie defense," and in 1979 a jury found White guilty only of involuntary manslaughter. When the verdict was announced, a riot erupted in San Francisco. Many people complained that the Twinkie defense had masked the jury's own prejudice against gays. (White, after spending some time in jail, committed suicide.)

No less controversial was the verdict handed down in June 1982 by a jury in Washington, D.C., that found John W. Hinckley,

John W. Hinckley, Jr., is led to a facility for psychiatric testing after shooting President Ronald Reagan in 1981. After Hinckley was acquitted of attempted murder charges on grounds of insanity, several states modified and restricted the insanity defense.

Jr., not guilty by reason of insanity in his attempted assassination in March 1981 of President Ronald Reagan and in the shooting of three other men. According to psychiatric testimony presented by defense attorneys, Hinckley, a 26-year-old college dropout from a wealthy Colorado family, was obsessed with the actress Jodie Foster and the role she played in *Taxi Driver*. In this 1976 film, Foster played a 12-year-old prostitute rescued by a gun-toting taxi driver who initially plans to kill a presidential candidate. The defense argued that Hinckley identified himself so closely with the taxi driver, played by Robert De Niro, that he was compelled to reenact the plot of the film.

Hinckley was acquitted and then confined indefinitely to an institution for the mentally ill, St. Elizabeth's Hospital in Washington, where he was treated for mental illness, with the understanding that his legal status would be reviewed every six months. In August 1988, his attending physicians withdrew an earlier request to the court that Hinckley be allowed a temporary leave from the hospital. Prosecutors had opposed the release because of what they called "disturbing entries" in Hinckley's treatment record at the hospital, including evidence that he had written a mail-order house for a nude sketch of Jodie Foster.

Hinckley's acquittal sparked a public outcry. Members of the U.S. Senate and the House of Representatives proposed 13 changes in the federal laws pertaining to the insanity defense. Many states also reacted forcefully. Idaho has eliminated the insanity defense, and Montana has limited it so severely that it scarcely exists on the books. California has also restricted the defense, and, as of 1989, four other states now allow juries to find a defendant guilty but mentally ill. Some 20 states have considered adding the guilty-but-mentally-ill plea to their criminal laws.

Who Is Insane?

Some critics of the insanity defense argue that *insanity* and *sanity* are legal, not medical or psychiatric, terms, and the law cannot precisely define insanity and has made no effort to define sanity. Persons whose bizarre behavior might cause the public to call them crazy could be—and often are—considered perfectly sane under the law.

A well-documented case is that of David Berkowitz, a 24-year-old former postal clerk who murdered 6 people and wounded 8 others in New York between July 1976 and August 1977. He later claimed he was told to commit the murders by a 6,000-year-old demon who spoke to him through the body of a dog owned by his neighbor Sam. Berkowitz called himself the Son of Sam—and was ruled legally sane. He pleaded guilty to murder in May 1978. As of 1989, he remained in prison.

Another objection raised by critics of the insanity defense is that the physicians who appear in court as "expert" witnesses often act as "hired guns," tailoring their professional judgment to suit the side that is paying them. These critics point to the custom in some European countries. There, physicians are summoned by the court, not one side of a case or the other, and asked to provide an impartial judgment about the medical aspects of the legal dispute. In the United States, the "adversary system" by which legal cases are resolved allows each side to have its own expert testify.

At least one survey of American judges suggests that they prefer the European practice in which "impartial" court-appointed medical witnesses testify in legal cases. The American College of Ob-

Serial killer David Berkowitz after his arrest in 1977. Berkowitz, also known as the Son of Sam killer, was judged to be legally sane and later pleaded guilty to six counts of first-degree murder.

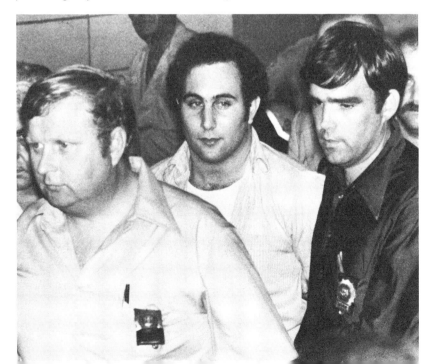

stetricians and Gynecologists, a group of doctors who specialize in the medical problems of women, polled 338 judges around the country and found that 84% of them favored the use of court-appointed medical experts in court cases, as is done in England. Some doctors also urge that a procedure be established whereby a panel of physicians would evaluate the credentials of all doctors who claim particular expertise in a given medical field.

•   •   •   •

CHAPTER 4

· · · · · · · · · · · · · ·

THE RIGHTS OF PATIENTS

Karen Ann Quinlan

"Life's perhaps the only riddle
That we shrink from giving up!"

—Sir W. S. Gilbert,
The Gondoliers (1889)

Every Fourth of July, Americans celebrate the birth of their nation and its Declaration of Independence, which announced that all men are owed the right to "life, liberty and the pursuit of happiness."

Those three rights lie at the heart of some of the major issues raised by laws concerning medicine: the right to begin and sustain life; the right to make decisions about one's life (and one's body); and the right to change those decisions if they make one unhappy. It was thus fitting that in 1976, the 200th anniversary of the Declaration of Independence, the New Jersey Supreme Court ruled in the case of Karen Ann Quinlan. She was a 21-year-old woman who was in an irreversible coma (caused by taking a combination of alcohol and tranquilizers) but was kept alive in a hospital on a respirator, a breathing machine, for nearly a year. Because doctors gave her no chance of recovery, her parents wanted her taken off the respirator and allowed to die. After a long court battle, a New Jersey judge agreed that a person's "right to privacy" permitted a patient—or someone acting on the behalf of a patient who is permanently unconscious—to authorize the end of life-sustaining procedures. Ironically, after the respirator was disconnected, Quinlan continued to breathe on her own for nine years. She died in June 1985, a full decade after she had lost consciousness. At any rate, this right-to-privacy decision had an immediate impact. In August 1976, Boston's Massachusetts General Hospital published guidelines for dividing critically ill patients into four treatment groups, ranging from Class A, those for whom "maximum [treatment] effort without reservation" should be used, to Class D, those patients so hopelessly ill that "all therapy can be discontinued . . . though maximum comfort" of the patient should be ensured.

CONSENT

The law has long recognized that each patient has the right to determine what will be done, or not done, to his or her body. As a writer for the American Association of Medical Assistants has put it, "Every person of sound mind is entitled to say whether he gets cut, by whom he gets cut, and where he gets cut."

The first American lawsuits concerning a patient's right to consent to or refuse medical treatment were tried in 1905, a year that saw two such cases. In one, an Illinois court ruled against a doctor who had operated on a woman without obtaining her specific consent to do so. In the other, a Minnesota court ordered a doctor to pay a patient $14,322—a huge amount at the time—for the same reason.

For the next five decades, the chief issue in such cases was whether a particular patient had freely and fully authorized the treatment a doctor performed. The matter became more complicated in the 1950s, when the courts first focused on the patient's understanding of the treatment being proposed; the likelihood of its success, and the consequences of refusing the treatment. Judges and juries held that physicians must fully explain the consequences of a proposed treatment and that a patient must decide to go ahead on the basis of "informed consent."

It is generally understood that in order to fulfill the obligation to inform the patient about a proposed treatment, a doctor must explain:

- the general nature of the treatment and its predictable results;
- the risks posed by the treatment and their chances of occurring;
- probable side effects and complications and their consequences;
- alternatives to the treatment—including doing nothing—and their likely outcomes.

If the proposed treatment is a high-risk one—such as radiation therapy—the patient should be told all about its potential problems, regardless of how upsetting that may be. But a doctor can withhold information from a patient if a complete description of the treatment will cause unnecessary upset or even harm and the potential risks of the treatment itself are not severe or are highly unlikely. In such cases, the doctor should explain the known risks and alternative treatments to the patient's spouse or closest relative.

The Rights of Teens

In the case of minors, the informed consent of at least one parent or guardian must be obtained by a doctor before treatment can be given. But, again, there are exceptions. One has to do with minors themselves. The law recognizes that some teenagers are mature enough to give informed consent, such as those teens who live apart from their parents and are financially independent of them. It is not always easy to determine when a minor is legally

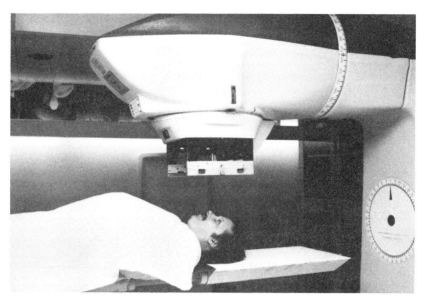

All state laws require that doctors inform patients undergoing radiation therapy of the procedure's potential side effects.

"mature," however; some 15 year olds are responsible, well-informed, and mature; some 20 year olds are not.

The courts have established three conditions that must be met before a teenager can be judged a mature minor, capable of giving informed consent to medical treatment: The minor must be near the age of majority (18, in most states) and appear to understand fully the nature and importance of the proposed treatment; the treatment must be intended for the minor's own benefit (not for that of another minor); and the treatment must pose no serious hazard and must also be considered necessary by conservative medical standards. (This can be confirmed by consulting another doctor.) Legal cases cite no specific age as being the cut-off point for "close to the age of majority," but Tom Christoffel, author of *Health and the Law: A Handbook for Health Professionals*, could not find a single lawsuit since the mid-1960s in which a doctor was ordered to pay monetary damages for treating a teenager over the age of 15 without parental consent.

Any self-supporting person under the age of 18 who lives separately from his or her parents is classified by the courts as an "emancipated minor" and is deemed capable of giving his or her own informed consent to medical treatment. And college students, although they often depend on the financial help of their parents, usually qualify as "emancipated minors" because they live apart from them.

There are other exceptions to the requirement that a doctor must secure the permission of the parents of a child or teenager before providing medical treatment. State laws often allow emergency treatment for a minor whose parents are not available to give consent. Many states also have passed laws allowing minors to be treated for sexually transmitted diseases without parental consent. Even in states that lack such a law, a doctor can often bypass parental consent and treat the teenager on the grounds that a medical emergency has arisen. Some states also allow doctors to give minors contraceptives without obtaining parental consent, and many permit minors to obtain medical treatment for a pregnancy without parental consent (though abortion is not always included among the treatments). In every state, doctors can treat minors for alcohol and drug addiction without the consent of the parents.

The Right to Say No

The right of a patient—either an adult or a minor—to approve treatment includes the right to order it stopped or to refuse it altogether. In particular, patients who are terminally ill—so sick that their illness will surely cause their death—have the right to "die with dignity" and refuse the use of any "heroic" measures that will not cure but only postpone their inevitable end. Many states have passed specific legislature involving these rights. For example, in September 1976, California passed the Natural Death Act, which gave patients the option of refusing treatment, life-prolonging treatment in particular.

When is it legally and morally acceptable to "pull the plug" and stop life-support treatment? In an effort to let patients make that crucial decision for themselves and in advance, 38 states and the District of Columbia have recently passed so-called living-will laws, enabling all persons to put into writing their wishes for the health-care treatment they should receive and the procedures that should be followed if they become terminally ill and are unable to tell their doctors or family what they want done.

Most living wills state that if life-sustaining procedures will simply prolong the dying process, they should not be used or should be stopped, and the person would then be allowed to die naturally, with medication and other medical procedures used only to ease pain and provide comfort. All living-will laws provide immunity from legal action to the health-care providers who follow the patient's requests, and many of the laws say a living will is only valid if the person is terminally ill. In some states, a living will is binding only if the person reaffirms it after being told that his or her condition is terminal, and in many states, a living will has to be reaffirmed periodically in order to be valid.

The question of when to allow a person to die naturally instead of keeping him or her alive by artificial means goes beyond deciding whether to keep a person who is permanently unconscious on a respirator. Karen Ann Quinlan's parents sought to have her disconnected from the machine that artificially assisted her breathing, but they did not ask as well that the needles and tubes that artificially supplied her with liquefied food and water be removed. Some legal and medical experts believe that there is no difference between artificially supplying oxygen and artificially supplying sustenance and that if it is legally permissible to disconnect one, it is also permissible to disconnect the other. Living-will laws and previous court rulings seem to concur with these experts.

When Is Someone Dead?

Along with the many complex issues crucial to right-to-die cases is what would appear to be a simple concern: determining when, exactly, a person is dead. In truth, however, the legal definition of death itself has become quite complicated. For centuries, death was said to occur when a person ceased to breathe and his or her heart ceased to beat. The ways of determining death were equally straightforward: feeling part of the body to find out if it was warm or cold; listening for a heartbeat; checking for a pulse (indicating the heart is still beating strongly enough to circulate blood); holding a mirror or a feather close to the person's mouth to see if any breath issued from it.

In most instances, these methods can still be used. But for hospitalized people whose bodily functions are being assisted by sophisticated medical technology, the question of when or whether death has occurred becomes far more difficult. Respirators and other artificial machines maintain essential body functions and thus blur the line separating life from death.

For this reason, the definition of death has expanded. It no longer means only a lack of spontaneous breathing and heartbeat; it also includes brain death, or an irreversible end to purposeful brain activity. And even this definition is complicated. Brain-dead patients have been sustained so successfully on heart and lung machines that other functions, such as digesting food and filtering wastes, can be maintained. In fact, this advanced technology has enabled the fetuses of brain-dead pregnant women to be nurtured for several weeks.

The debate over establishing a useful definition of death led a committee at the Harvard Medical School to recommend in 1968 that four specific tests be applied to determine whether a person in an irreversible coma is alive or dead. The tests should show whether the person lacks awareness of externally applied stimuli (such as pinpricks); lacks the ability to breathe spontaneously (that is, without the aid of a respirator); lacks reflex responses; and lacks brain activity as measured by an electroencephalograph (EEG), a machine that measures electrical impulses in the brain.

The committee also recommended that if a person failed to respond to all these tests, a day should be allowed to go by before trying them again. If the result was the same, then the person could be declared dead. Some doctors now think the 24-hour waiting period is unnecessarily long, so some states have shortened it.

The Harvard guidelines paved the way for new state laws dealing with death. Kansas took the lead in the early 1970s, and 25 states followed suit, updating their statutes to reflect the latest definitions of death. In 1978, the National Conference on Uniform State Laws proposed the Uniform Brain Death Act; in 1979, the American Medical Association proposed another law. In 1981, the Law Reform Commission of Canada came up with its own act, the Uniform Determination of Death Act, which both the AMA and the American Bar Association (ABA), the largest national lawyers' group, decided was better than those that each had proposed earlier. As a result, the Canadian model law has now been passed in 17 states and the District of Columbia.

Organ Donors

The debate over the definition of death stems in part from the growing need for body parts such as kidneys, hearts, the corneas of eyes, and lungs to be used in transplant operations. Because the donors are usually people who have just died, there has been an effort to standardize the laws regarding the removal of vital organs. It resulted in a model law passed in one form or another by virtually every state: the Uniform Anatomical Gift Act. It states that any person 18 years of age or older and of sound mind can authorize the removal of any part of his or her body after death and have it go to any hospital, doctor, dentist, or medical school for the purpose of education, research, therapy, or transplantation. The body parts also can be given to a storage facility, or bank (such as a so-called eye bank), where they can be kept under refrigeration for future use.

People who wish to donate parts of their body after their death can state this in their will or can sign a uniform donor card in the presence of two witnesses. In 43 states, they can give such permission just by checking off a box on their driver's license. In most states, people also may change their mind about donating their body parts and may then revoke the gift by destroying the donor card or telling two witnesses that they have withdrawn authorization for removal of the body parts.

In an effort to increase the number of organs available for transplant operations, several states, including New York and Maryland, have passed "required-request" laws. These state that when a person has been declared brain dead, the hospital is required to ask his or her family to donate the patient's organs to someone whom they might keep alive. In 1987, the federal government passed a similar law. A severe shortage of donor organs still exists, however.

EUTHANASIA

Another controversy surrounds the issue of euthanasia, or "mercy killing." This issue arises when a family member or a doctor deliberately takes the life or assists in the suicide of a gravely ill person in order to end his or her misery.

Organizations in the United States, Japan, England, Australia, Germany, France, Spain, and a dozen other countries urge the acceptance of voluntary euthanasia and the passage of laws permitting it, but as of 1989 only Holland had adopted a "noncriminal aid-in-dying" law, making "euthanasia . . . a fact of life and a way of death," as correspondent Ed Bradley reported on the CBS news program "60 Minutes."

The word *euthanasia* (which combines the ancient Greek words for "good" and "death") has been used to mean a variety of things. Some people distinguish passive euthanasia, in which no specific measures are taken to end a patient's life, from active euthanasia, in which concrete steps are taken—such as injecting a fatal dose of medicine—to end a person's life. Voluntary euthanasia refers to the preference for death over painful, incurable illness; nonvoluntary euthanasia happens when a patient who is comatose or otherwise incapable of making a decision is killed for reasons of mercy. On the other hand, if a very ill person expresses a desire to continue living and is nevertheless killed, that is considered "involuntary" euthanasia in moral terms and just plain murder in legal terms.

Suicide itself was once a crime—punished, when unsuccessful, by death in some cases. In early 19th-century England, for example, people who made unsuccessful suicide attempts were nursed back to health so that they could be hanged. Although the English law making suicide itself a crime was abolished in 1961, it is still against the law—in both England and the United States—to help someone take his or her own life.

Doctors polled by the AMA in June 1988 showed that a majority would honor a request to remove all life-support systems, including food and water, from hopelessly ill or irreversibly comatose patients. They would thus engage in either passive or voluntary euthanasia. More than two thirds of the doctors contacted by the AMA in a telephone survey reported that they had received at least one such request.

Yet the same month that the poll was taken, the 420 members of the AMA's House of Delegates, the policy-making group for the entire 300,000-member organization, passed a resolution that opposed mercy killing. According to the chairman of the board of trustees of the doctors' group, the organization firmly believed that euthanasia "is wrong . . . and the medical profession will continue to deplore it."

This AMA action was prompted by the controversy that erupted in January 1988 when the *Journal of the American Medical Association* (JAMA) published an anonymous article on the subject. Written by a young doctor, it described how he had given a fatal injection to "Debbie," a gravely ill cancer patient who had said to him, "Let's get this over with." Was this voluntary euthanasia, or was it assisting a suicide? As the AMA's board chairman observed, the debate over euthanasia "will be with society for the foreseeable future." Indeed, a 1987 survey of 1,250 adults found that 57% approved of doctors using euthanasia when asked to do so by terminally ill patients who are in great pain.

Even so, those who participate in what they may deem as voluntary euthanasia are tried—and often sentenced—as criminals. In 1985, Roswell Gilbert, a 76-year-old resident of Broward County, Florida, was sentenced to life in prison after being convicted of first-degree murder in the mercy killing of his wife, to whom he had been married for 51 years and who was gravely ill. His appeal for clemency was turned down, and he remains in prison.

Baby Doe

Euthanasia is not an issue just for the elderly. In 1983, a furor arose when the federal Department of Health and Human Services established the Baby Doe rules, which were later revised and finally invalidated by the U.S. Supreme Court in 1988. These rules sought to force hospitals and doctors to provide treatment to seriously handicapped newborn babies, even if their parents and physicians opposed it.

Once again, an issue has been complicated by advances in medical technology. Infants who would have died had they been born in the 1950s or early 1960s can now often survive for long periods with the help of the sophisticated, though costly, medical treatment available in the neonatal intensive care units (NICUs) found in some 600 hospitals across the country. As of 1989, these units had treated 200,000 newborn babies each year at an estimated annual cost of $1.5 billion.

As a result, parents, doctors, and the courts must decide when, if ever, it is justifiable not to provide life-prolonging treatment to babies with severe mental and physical disabilities; when, if ever, a baby is too young, too small, or too afflicted to be saved by this new technology; and how often and in what specific kinds

Police surround the body of a suicide victim. It is against the law to help a person take his or her own life.

of cases does medical treatment cause more harm than good.

Baby Doe was a severely retarded child born in Bloomington, Indiana, in 1982, with a blocked esophagus, which made it impossible for her to eat normally. Her parents and the attending physician, feeling that their child was so severely handicapped that she could never lead a healthy life, rejected surgery that would have corrected the esophogus problem, and the hospital— citing state laws against child abuse and neglect—asked a court to intervene. The court ruled that the parents, who had been told by other doctors that the corrective surgery was possible, were nevertheless not being "neglectful" when they decided against it. The child later died while the case was still before an appeals court.

The Reagan administration decided that the Indiana court's ruling violated a federal law designed to prohibit discrimination against handicapped persons, and it issued the Baby Doe rules to warn hospitals that they could lose federal funds unless they put up posters throughout their facilities stating that it was against federal law to fail to feed and care for handicapped infants.

The American Hospital Association and other health-care groups opposed the new rules, which finally went into effect in February 1984. Then in a New York lawsuit (*United States v.*

Roswell Gilbert after he was found guilty of first-degree murder in the "mercy killing" of his wife. Gilbert, whose wife was gravely ill, was nonetheless sentenced to life imprisonment.

University Hospital) involving Baby Jane Doe, a severely handicapped newborn girl, a federal court ruled that the federal law protecting handicapped infants had not meant to apply to treatment decisions involving seriously ill newborn babies. The U.S. Supreme Court upheld that ruling in 1986.

The issue is hardly resolved, however. In 1984, Congress revised the federal child-abuse laws to require that all handicapped newborns receive the medical treatment they need unless they are dying or irreversibly comatose, or unless the treatment would not help or would prove inhumane.

CONFIDENTIALITY

Medical tradition and modern law both require doctors to keep secret whatever their patients tell them. In the 5th century B.C., Hippocrates established this rule of confidentiality by directing new doctors to pledge: "Whatsoever things I see or hear . . . in any attendance on the sick . . . which ought not to be noised about, I will keep silent thereon, counting such things to be professional secrets." Centuries later, the AMA reiterated that principle in its code of ethics, which declared that physicians "shall respect the rights of patients . . . and shall safeguard patient confidences within the constraints of the law."

Pledges of confidentiality are an issue because doctors and other health-care providers often cannot treat patients without first learning the most personal, intimate, and potentially embarrassing details of their life. For their part, patients often would not discuss these matters if they thought the information might become public. By and large, doctors carefully guard such confidences, and few lawsuits have ever been filed by patients who contend that their confidentiality was violated.

In spite of this good record, many states have passed laws stating that if a doctor betrays a professional secret, his or her license may be suspended or revoked. In Michigan, this breach is considered a crime and is punishable by a fine, imprisonment, or both. And 36 states and the District of Columbia prohibit doctors from testifying in court about a patient unless the patient agrees, is on trial for murder, or has used the insanity plea.

Exceptions to the Rule

Some laws require doctors to reveal confidential information. These public-reporting statutes assist authorities with a variety of purposes: containing the spread of contagious, infectious, and dangerous diseases such as pneumonia, tuberculosis, measles, chicken pox, cholera, yellow fever, or malaria; compiling vital statistics concerning births and deaths; combating child neglect and abuse; and reporting criminally inflicted wounds such as those resulting from shootings and stabbings.

Courts have also ruled that a doctor has a professional responsibility to disclose information about patients who pose a threat to others. In a 1976 case in California, a psychologist learned from his patient, a college student, that he might physically harm his former girlfriend. The psychologist tried unsuccessfully to have the patient committed to a mental hospital, but he never warned the police or the young woman, whom the patient ultimately murdered. When the parents of the murdered woman brought the case to trial, the California Supreme Court ruled that the therapist had a duty to protect a threatened person, if necessary by revealing what the patient had said in confidence. Similar rulings have since occurred in other state courts.

AIDS and Confidentiality

Another issue concerning confidentiality is the AIDS epidemic. As of 1989, a substantial percentage of AIDS victims are drug addicts and male homosexuals, two groups ostracized by much of the public. For this reason, members of these groups who contract the fatal virus resist having information about their condition revealed to anyone outside a limited group of health-care providers. The trouble is that this confidentiality hampers the efforts of those who are working to stop the spread of AIDS and to find a cure for it, because much remains to be learned about how AIDS is spread and how it develops. (To date, doctors believe AIDS can be spread only through the exchange of blood, semen, and other bodily fluids, not by casual contact, such as shaking hands or hugging.)

Another issue involves life-insurance companies that have begun requiring applicants for policies to take a blood test to determine if they have been exposed to the fatal AIDS virus. In 1986, the city council of Washington, D.C., passed a law prohibiting local health- and life-insurance firms from screening applicants in this way. As a result, many companies stopped issuing policies. The U.S. Congress, which regulates city funding in Washington, ordered changes in the council's law, and in late 1988, the council began working on them. Washington's law regarding insurance firms was the strictest of its kind, but a number of states have passed or considered passing similar legislation, including Maine, California, Florida, Wisconsin, Massachusetts, Michigan, and New York.

In June 1986, the U.S. Justice Department decreed that employers could discriminate against AIDS victims based on the fear that other workers may have of catching the disease, even if the fear is not "reasonable." Since then, 15 states have passed laws declaring AIDS a handicap, thereby placing it under the existing statutes that prohibit discrimination against handicapped people. In all, health officials in 34 states have said they would respond to complaints of discrimination based on AIDS.

And in 1987, a Supreme Court ruling (*Florida v. Arline*) gave an expansive reading to the federal law barring discrimination against the handicapped; many believe that this case ruling has benefited many AIDS victims who would otherwise have been excluded from school or lost their jobs. This prompted the Justice Department to change its position in October 1988.

PUBLIC HEALTH

Ever since public-health law became a central issue in the 19th century, there have been efforts to restrict, alter, or encourage activities that may affect the safety of individuals and also society at large. Some laws devised for these purposes have been challenged by citizens who believe their personal liberty has been wrongly restricted. On occasion, judges agree and rule that the law in question is unconstitutional; at other times, the courts uphold the law, deciding that the limits imposed on a person's behavior are justified in order to protect his or her own safety, as well as the safety of others.

The Princess of Wales greets an AIDS patient in a New York hospital. The issue of AIDS and confidentiality is controversial. Some believe that victims of the disease should not have to disclose their condition to any-one but specific health-care providers. Others argue that this restriction will prevent scientists from learning more about the virus.

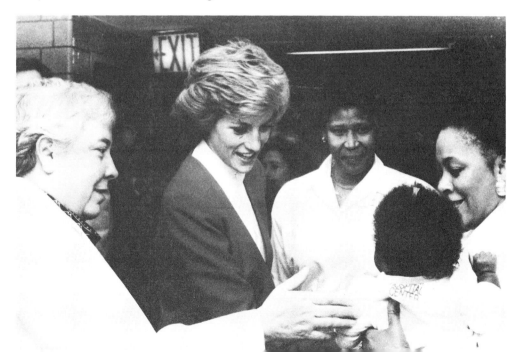

Some of the oldest laws on record provide for a quarantine—or an order of isolation—to be put on a person, place, or group for the purpose of keeping diseases from spreading. The power of governments to impose quarantines is upheld by the courts as long as medical evidence shows that the danger is real and as long as personal freedom is restricted as minimally as possible. Courts have ruled that states can prohibit public gatherings, compel people to stay in their homes, and even "hold and treat" a person who has an infectious disease that poses a danger to public health.

MENTAL-HEALTH LAW

Since the late 1960s, the legal role of physicians who specialize in mental health has grown to such an extent that an entire new field has been created: mental-health law. Judges have become increasingly involved in regulating what some legal experts call "the public practice of psychiatry," ruling in many cases on the constitutionality and even the correctness of committing people to mental hospitals for treatment, as well as on what kind of treatment they should receive and whether they can refuse all treatment if they wish.

As recently as the late 1970s, it was a routine matter to commit someone to a mental hospital without his or her consent. It was seldom challenged by the courts, and little practical consideration was given to a person's right to refuse medical treatment. But a new trend is developing. People are seldom sent to mental hospitals against their will merely on the direction of one or two doctors. Indeed, two thirds of the states have revised their mental-health laws to provide for procedural safeguards and for establishing a more specific basis for commitment.

Legal grounds for involuntary commitment still exist, however. The state can invoke its "police power" to protect society from people who might be dangerous. The state can also act as a sort of "parent" under the concept known as *parens patriae* and function as "the general guardian of all infants, idiots and lunatics." Sometimes the state will act under a combination of both principles.

There are two types of civil commitment hearings. Some states require an initial hearing to determine if there is "probable cause," or sufficient evidence, to warrant putting a person in a mental hospital. All states require that a "final" hearing be held, presided over by a judge or panel (of doctors or other medical experts) that decides whether an involuntary commitment is justified. Some states call for the person to have legal representation at a civil commitment hearing and in some cases require that a person with no money be given free legal counsel. The U.S. Supreme Court has ruled that whatever standard is applied by a court or a panel to determine whether a person should be committed involuntarily, the evidence proving it must be "clear and convincing."

All states also allow for the short-term "emergency" commitment of persons to mental hospitals. This contingency plan is often invoked. Indeed, according to Tom Christoffel's *Health and the Law: A Handbook for Health Professionals*, some experts contend that "the so-called emergency procedure is, in almost every state, the *standard* procedure and almost everyone is hospitalized, initially, under the emergency procedure, whether there is an emergency or not." The length of the "short-term" hospitalization permitted under "emergency" conditions ranges among the states from two weeks to two months.

Under most state laws, even people who voluntarily agree to be admitted to a mental institution are not free to leave it whenever they wish. They usually must stay in the hospital for a waiting period of 5 to 30 days after asking to be released. And they will be let out only if the hospital does not start commitment proceedings of its own during that waiting period.

A "need for treatment" is usually not sufficient grounds for institutionalization. Instead, judges and panels tend to require proof that a person poses a threat of physical danger to him- or herself or others, based on recent examples of dangerous actions or threats. It is not easy, however, to predict how dangerous someone is. Critics of the civil-commitment process hold that because mental-health professionals, who are often more concerned about letting a dangerous person go free than about infringing on the liberty of a harmless person, play it safe by "overpredicting" the threat of danger. These critics maintain that medical experts, instead of weighing the evidence, "flip coins in the courtroom."

A Different Law for Minors

Although new safeguards have helped protect adults from being involuntarily committed to a mental institution, teenagers and young children have fewer rights.

If parents authorize a minor to be committed, the minor is considered a voluntary patient no matter how strongly he or she objects and is thus denied many of the procedural safeguards that protect adults, including a judicial hearing. This is the case, even though some studies have shown that a parent's decision to authorize the commitment of a child frequently occurs because of the parent's problems (including mental illness), not the child's.

In 1979, the U.S. Supreme Court ruled that parents may commit a minor to a mental hospital not only without the child's consent but also without any kind of court hearing; they need only an evaluation by a mental-health professional. The specific case in question involved very young children, however, and as of 1989 it was still not known exactly how the ruling would affect the rights of teenagers.

In spite of the Supreme Court's finding, state legislatures have passed a variety of laws designed to protect children and teenagers from being committed "voluntarily," but really against their will. The laws governing the commitment of children are state statutes and differ from state to state. In Hawaii, a parent may authorize only the commitment of children who are under the age of 15; in Pennsylvania, the cutoff age is 14. In Washington State, a child over the age of 13 must consent to be committed, and in West Virginia, children over 12 must be asked for consent.

When reviewing or writing future laws, state legislators will probably take into consideration the opinion issued by Chief Justice Warren Burger in 1979: "Simply because the decision of a parent is not agreeable to a child or because it involves risks does not automatically transfer the power to make that decision from the parents to some agency or officer of the state. . . . Most children, even in adolescence, simply are not able to make sound judgments concerning many decisions, including their need for medical care or treatment. Parents can and must make those judgments."

●   ●   ●   ●

CHAPTER 5

· · · · · · · · · · · · ·

WHO GOES FIRST?

Surgeon General C. Everett Koop at a press conference for AIDS education.

"After you, my dear Alphonse."
"No, after you, my dear Gaston."

—F. B. Opper,
"Alphonse and Gaston" comic strip

In a way, everything a doctor does for a patient is an experiment. Every person is different, and a particular patient's response to a treatment can never be known until it is tried.

"Human experimentation began when the first doctors treated the first patients," wrote Lawrence K. Altman, M.D., a medical reporter for the *New York Times*. However, doctors made little effort to record the results of their experiments until about 200 years ago. Sometimes their first guinea pigs were themselves. As Altman writes in his book on the topic, *Who Goes First?*, self-experimentation "has been, and *continues* to be, a medical tradition."

Many breakthroughs in the history of medicine began as experiments doctors performed on themselves. Physicians subjected themselves, for example, to the various anesthetics that put patients to sleep or block their pain, thus making modern surgery possible. Doctors also experimented on themselves with many of the vaccines that prevent the spread of deadly or crippling diseases and with cures that correct birth defects in children or heart damage in adults.

From the discovery of anesthetics in the mid-1800s to the battle against AIDS today, human experimentation has been vital to medical progress. Even actions one hardly thinks about—swallowing a pill, getting a shot, drinking purified water—originated as medical experiments performed on humans. Animals are often used in the first research stages, but ultimately all medical theories or new medicines must be tested on humans.

A HISTORY OF ABUSE

In spite of all the good that human experimentation has accomplished, most judges in the United States and elsewhere have long distrusted human experiments that have come to light in legal cases. They have a very good reason—namely, the history of atrocities committed against unsuspecting "victims to science." Such abuses became widespread between World War I and World War II. According to one doctor who worked in Europe during that period, "New drugs, new experimental surgical procedures were commonly tested on charity patients, who rarely understood what was being done to them. Often they were . . . [permanently injured] or killed—experimental 'animals' sacrificed in the interests of medical progress."

Dr. Daniel Zagury of the Marie and Pierre Curie University in Paris injected himself with an untested AIDS vaccine and suffered no ill effects. Zagury's experiment has not yet led to an effective treatment.

World War II Atrocities

As appalling and unforgivable as those human experiments were, they paled beside the crimes Nazi doctors—some of them schooled at the best universities and once highly regarded—committed against the helpless prisoners of Nazi concentration camps or that Japanese researchers committed against thousands of prisoners of war over an even longer period of time. Public revelations of these atrocities—in the case of the Japanese experiments, more than 35 years after they were discovered—shocked the world.

Nazi doctors locked concentration camp prisoners in airtight chambers and then rapidly changed the air pressure to simulate the conditions an airplane pilot might experience if he fell from a great height without oxygen or a parachute. Researchers also deliberately infected prisoners with cholera, diphtheria, smallpox, yellow fever, and other deadly diseases in order to test experimental and largely useless vaccines on the victims. They even injected prisoners with gasoline to see how long they would survive. Most died in less than a minute.

One well-known expert on malaria—a former member of an international commission that studied this disease—infected more than 1,000 concentration camp prisoners with it and then gave them huge doses of experimental drugs, killing more than 400. After the war, at a trial in Nuremberg, Germany, 15 out of the 23 Nazi doctors accused of crimes against humanity were convicted, and 7 of them—including the malaria expert—were hanged.

American officials learned of similarly horrible experiments that Japanese researchers conducted on Chinese and American war prisoners between 1931, when the Japanese first invaded China, and 1945, when World War II ended. Japanese doctors froze the body parts of living humans in order to test methods of thawing them out; exposed a person's liver to prolonged X rays; pumped bodies full of horse blood; and dissected a living person.

The Nuremberg Code

In 1947, the special court that had ruled on the German war crimes drew up the Nuremberg Code, 10 principles that doctors and researchers around the world were urged to follow. It stated that human experiments "yield results for the good of society that are unprocurable by other methods or means of study" but that certain moral, ethical, and legal principles must be observed when such experiments were conducted.

All human subjects must not only agree to the experiments but must be mentally "competent" to do so. The experiment must also be explained to them in terms they understand. The code specified further that human experiments must provide important information that cannot be obtained otherwise and should also

- be justified by earlier studies, laboratory tests, and experiments on animals;
- minimize the subjects' suffering and injury;
- involve no risk of a disabling injury or death;
- produce a benefit that is comparable to the risk undertaken in the experiment;
- be based on proper preparation;
- be performed by qualified people;

- allow the subjects to stop the experiment whenever they want;
- be conducted by a researcher prepared to stop the experiment if there is a good chance of harming the patient.

Strong as the Nuremberg Code was, it lacked the authority of international law. Thus, in 1964, the World Medical Association issued the Helsinki Declaration, following a meeting in the Finnish capital, which added new guidelines. Still, the only enforcers of humane experimentation are doctors and researchers, whose duty it is to obtain the informed consent of their subjects.

An Ugly American Chapter

Human experimentation continues to arouse controversy. In 1972, news surfaced that for some 40 years, the U.S. Public Health Service had been conducting a "study in nature" of untreated syphilis, a potentially fatal venereal disease, among rural black men in the South. The aim of this study was to follow the natural course of the disease; the subjects, who had been asked to volunteer, were given free medical care for other ailments and promised free burials. But researchers working on the Tuskegee study, as it came to be known (it was conducted at the Tuskegee Institute in Alabama), never told the subjects that they were being examined as part of an experiment, and the subjects were never given effective treatment, even after such treatment became available in the early 1950s. Worse, the men were steered away from the cure if they tried to get it on their own.

The Tuskegee study began around 1932, long before the Nuremberg Code or the Helsinki Declaration, but it continued long after both those documents were issued. Only in 1973, after word of the experiments reached and outraged the public, did the experimenters end their study. A suit was initiated by surviving families of subjects who had died during the study; living subjects still afflicted with syphilis; and subjects who did not suffer from the disease. They received payments ranging from $5,000 to $37,500.

Not long after this episode, evidence emerged that researchers employed by the U.S. Army had conducted chemical and drug experiments on human subjects after World War II without the subjects' knowledge or consent. One researcher uncovered 50 unethical medical studies, including one in which penicillin, an antibiotic drug, was withheld from 109 servicemen whose infections might have been cured by it, thus exposing them to the risk of getting rheumatic fever. In another experiment, patients suffering from severe cirrhosis, a serious liver disease, were treated with useless chemicals. In still another study, 26 newborn babies were exposed to extensive X rays so their urinary bladder functions could be studied.

It also was discovered that military officials had once purposely ordered that germs and other toxic substances be spread through eight areas of the country in order to conduct a mock germ warfare attack. At one point, a poison was spread through two New York City subway lines. It was further disclosed that officials at the Central Intelligence Agency (CIA) had secretly experimented on uninformed subjects with mind-altering drugs, including the hallucinogen LSD. One subject, an army doctor who had unwittingly consumed LSD in an after-dinner drink, suffered a bad trip (drug-induced experience), became depressed, and later committed suicide.

In 1980, a lawsuit was filed by nine former patients of a prominent Canadian psychiatrist who had given them heavy doses of LSD and electroshock therapy as part of secret CIA experiments in mind control in the 1950s. The former patients, alleging permanent brain damage and other disorders, reportedly obtained a settlement totaling $750,000 in damages.

REGULATING ABUSES

One reason these horror stories caused such alarm was that the U.S. government had taken measures to ensure against them once it became involved in biomedical (biological and medical) research. This involvement skyrocketed after World War II. In 1947, 2 years after the war ended, the federal government spent $27 million on medical research. By 1952, the sum was $103 million, and by 1962, that amount had increased sixfold. In 1973, federal research funds topped $2.25 billion.

This growth spawned more rigorous rules and laws meant to protect human subjects, especially vulnerable ones such as minors, prison inmates, the mentally incompetent, institutionalized persons, and the chronically ill. Federal regulation of biomedical research has been handled mostly by the Department of Health and Human Services with powers it obtained under the Public Health Services Act, a law passed by Congress.

The federal Food and Drug Administration also has the power to establish standards for the research and experiments done to test the safety and effectiveness of medications. In fact, the FDA requires extensive experiments on humans before any drug or medical device can be sold to the public. The FDA has the power under the Food, Drug and Cosmetics Act to require that informed consent to an experiment be obtained from all human subjects on whom tests of new drugs are to be made. The FDA also requires hospitals and other medical facilities to impanel an institutional review board (IRB) that approves all proposed experiments of new drugs on people in that institution.

The Role of IRBs

In 1953, the National Institutes of Health (NIH) began the first federal regulation of experiments on humans by requiring that before any research involving humans could be conducted at the NIH Clinical Center in Bethesda, Maryland, the proposed experiment must win approval of a review committee.

In 1966, the surgeon general of the U.S. Public Health Service (PHS) cast a wider net, requiring reviews of all research supported by money from the PHS or other federal grants. Then, in 1974, Congress passed the National Research Act, which created the National Commission for the Protection of Human Subjects of Biomedical and Behavioral Research. Its responsibilities include investigating proposed experiments and making recommendations about them.

In 1981, the commission established additional regulations. It stipulated that screening proposals is not enough; once experiments are under way, IRBs must continue to monitor them. More than 500 medical institutions in the United States each now have one or more IRBs that function in this way.

Each IRB consists of at least five people of varying background and experience, including at least one person who has a non-scientific background and one who is in no way associated with the institution where the experiments are to take place. The IRB will not approve a research project unless it is convinced the risks to the human subjects are minimal and reasonable given the medical benefits the research is expected to produce.

The IRB also ensures that the rights and welfare of the subjects are protected and that they give their informed consent before an experiment begins. It is important that subjects have time to think about what they are getting into and that they do not feel railroaded into participating.

This last consideration is especially crucial in the case of prison inmates, "the perfect human guinea pigs," according to Tom Christoffel's *Health and the Law*. What makes them "perfect" is also the source of the problem. By definition, prison inmates are forced to remain inside a prison and obey its rules, which casts a doubt on their supposedly "voluntary" agreement to participate in medical experiments.

For this reason, many countries have passed laws that limit the use of prisoners as research subjects, and the United States has cut back on this research in recent years. Indeed, in 1982 Christoffel, an expert on medicine and the law, found it "likely that no prison research will be conducted in the future" in the United States. This opinion is based on the Presidential Commission for the Study of Ethical Problems in Medicine and Biomedical and Behavioral Research, which called for human subjects to be given adequate living accommodations.

Some medical researchers think children should never be used as subjects in medical experiments, but many new drugs and new medical procedures meant for children—such as certain vaccines—simply cannot be tested on adult volunteers. The presidential commission decided that medical research can be performed on children provided that their parents agree to it and the child does, too, assuming he or she is capable of understanding what the experiment involves. Most children seven years of age or older are considered capable of such understanding.

The States

Few states have passed laws about the use of human subjects in medical research. Those that did based the regulations on federal

statutes. When California passed such a law in 1978, its legislature noted that because neither the Nuremberg Code nor the
Helsinki Declaration could be legally enforced, a state law was
considered necessary. The California law established an "experimental subject's bill of rights" and set up criminal and civil
penalties for researchers who fail to secure the informed consent
of a potential subject.

When research poses grave risks, some courageous physicians
choose to act as subjects themselves. But this is not always an
option. For example, the surgeons who developed artificial hearts
could not possibly have operated on themselves and put an artificial heart in their own chest. And given the great risks involved,
neither a hospital review panel nor the FDA was likely to approve
the use of a healthy human in such an experiment, although
there were volunteers, including a 60-year-old widow and 3 inmates on death row. (The inmates suggested the artificial heart
could simply be turned off on the day of their execution.)

The potential benefit of experiments can outweigh even grave
risks in the case of certain subjects, who already face imminent
death. For this reason, the terminally ill are allowed to volunteer
for such experiments, as did dentist Barney Clark, a critically ill
heart patient who lived for several months after becoming the
first human to have an artificial heart implanted in his chest in
1982. Had the mechanical heart not been tried, he would most
likely have died much sooner.

EXPERIMENTING ON ANIMALS

For centuries, medical researchers have usually tested their theories on animals before experimenting with humans. Indeed, the
Nuremberg Code, mentioned above, requires that this be done.
Researchers use animals in many different sorts of experiments.
Some gather basic information; others apply that information
toward the treatment of specific illnesses; still others test new
drugs and chemicals on them. Vaccines and other medicines are
first tried out on animals, and some laboratory animals are used
to diagnose diseases in humans or in other animals. Animals also
are of use to students, who dissect them to learn about biology.

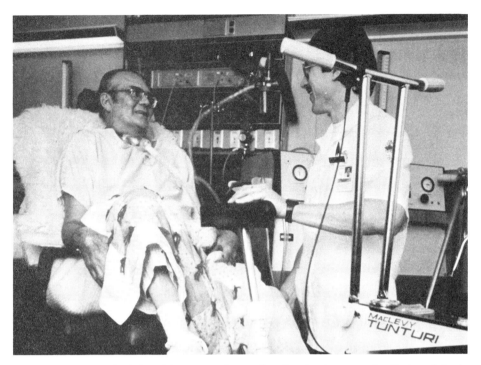

Barney Clark lived for several months after he became the first recipient of an artificial heart.

Animal Rights

Some organizations and individuals strongly oppose the use of animals in experiments, charging that it is both immoral and cruel. Antivivisection societies, made up of people who oppose the use of animals in surgical and other tests, have long been advocates of what newer groups now call animal rights.

In the United States, medical research using animals is regulated by federal, state, and local laws. A 1966 federal law, the Laboratory Animal Welfare Act, was passed in response to reports that pet dogs were being kidnapped and sold to medical research facilities. The law has been strengthened. It is now called the Animal Welfare Act (AWA). It provides for the U.S. secretary of agriculture to establish humane standards for the sale, transportation, handling, care, and treatment of laboratory animals. The Department of Agriculture also has the power to inspect all facilities that use live animals in research, tests, or experiments, except for elementary and secondary schools. Fines can be slapped on facilities that snub the rules.

The law also calls for research procedures to minimize the pain and distress suffered by the animals during the experiments. Critics of the law note, however, that it does not cover rats and mice, the most commonly used creatures, and that the inspection service of the Department of Agriculture is poorly funded and seldom imposes fines.

Getting Serious

The U.S. Public Health Service, a federal agency that provides most of the money used for approved biomedical research projects, has established nine detailed standards for the treatment of animals used in experiments. Its 1984 booklet, the *Guide for the Care and Use of Laboratory Animals*, demonstrated that the federal government has become concerned about keeping track of the experiments conducted on animals, although some critics believe that the government does not follow through on enforcement.

Thus, some animal-protection groups began to lobby state legislatures. In recent years, dozens of proposed laws have been submitted to state lawmakers, who have rejected most of them. In Massachusetts, however, a law was passed in 1983 that prohibits the operators of animal shelters from donating animals to research facilities or animal dealers. The law also bans researchers from importing animals from out-of-state shelters.

Animal research has also become a subject of international concern. The Council for International Organizations of Medical Science, a group sponsored by the World Health Organization (WHO) and by the United Nations, has issued a lengthy list of principles for conducting biomedical research using animals. It reiterates many points made in the U.S. government booklet.

Key Cases

Animal-rights advocates have waged their struggle in local courtrooms, schoolrooms, and laboratories. For example, groups have argued that students in junior and senior high schools, as well as those in college biology courses, can learn about living organisms without dissecting animals. They also have gathered information on science fair projects that they say have involved the abuse of animals.

Activists have had mixed success in the courtroom. An important case occurred in Maryland, where an appeals court ruled in 1983 that a researcher who cut some of the nerves in monkeys in order to study methods for treating humans who had suffered strokes was not violating the state's law against cruelty to animals. However, the U.S. Public Health Service decided the scientist did not abide by its rules on animal research and stopped funds for his project.

Another case involved the Animal Liberation Front, a group that burglarized a research laboratory at the University of Pennsylvania in 1984, destroying documents and stealing videotapes that showed experiments conducted on baboons. The break-in was illegal, but the evidence it brought to light caused the research facility to be fined $4,000 for giving the baboons insufficient anesthetic and for using unsanitary surgical procedures. Also in 1984, the Department of Agriculture fined the University of California at Berkeley $12,000 for not meeting federal requirements for animal research facilities.

In 1988, a complex issue arose when animal-rights groups complained that chimpanzees, a dwindling breed, were being used for AIDS research. As the *Washington Post* reported, "The question some animal conservationists ask is, can we afford to risk wiping out the world's chimpanzee population in our attempt to beat the AIDS threat? (Chimpanzees are the only species other than humans that can be infected with the human immunodeficiency virus.) The question some scientists ask—but only privately— is, can we afford not to?"

The debate heated up in 1988 when a study prepared on behalf of the National Academy of Sciences declared that humans are morally obligated to use animals for medical research. The study held that the aggressive tactics of the animal-rights movement threatened to delay or stop important medical advances. "The scientific community is being attacked by terrorist groups [that are] committing criminal acts, violating private property, defam-

A baby chimpanzee clings to its mother's back. The experiments some AIDS researchers have performed on chimpanzees, the only species aside from humans susceptible to the virus, have upset some animal-rights activists.

ing researchers," a member of the study group told the press. "It is the job of humans to care for each other . . . and in the end humans are more responsible to each other than to animals," he said. The study, which was funded by the National Institutes of Health and pharmaceutical companies, added that animals abandoned in pounds and shelters and threatened with being put to sleep anyway should instead be used in research.

Animal research is as essential as human research—but it is just as essential that both be performed properly, with caution, care, and compassion. As is the case in so many issues involving medicine and the law, a compromise must be reached and a balance maintained. Society must encourage scientific breakthroughs that will benefit many people. It must also preserve the rights and well-being of experimental subjects, human and animal, whose sacrifices make those breakthroughs possible.

•   •   •   •

CHAPTER 6

· · · · · · · · · · · ·

LAWYERS V. DOCTORS

Dr. Kronkhite: *Have you had this condition before?*
Patient: *Yes.*
Dr. Kronkhite: *Well, you've got it again.*

—Smith and Dale,
vaudeville comedians

Comedy writers can usually get a laugh with jokes about incompetent doctors. (Kronkhite, in the joke above, is a play
on the German word *Krankheit*, which means "illness.") In fact,

The 18th-century jurist William Blackstone wrote about medical malpractice in his book Commentaries on the Laws of England.

there is nothing funny about malpractice, which is why patients often sue doctors who have given them improper or inadequate treatment.

The first recorded medical malpractice case occurred in England in the 13th century, though the word malpractice (literally, bad practice) did not appear in a medical book until 1671. William Blackstone's *Commentaries on the Laws of England*, published in 1765, mentions a malpractice case decided by an English court in 1694. Exactly 100 years later, in 1794, the first malpractice case in America was tried in Connecticut.

EARLY HISTORY

In the United States, malpractice suits were rare for many years. The second case was not recorded in the United States until 1812, and 20 more years passed before the third occurred. One legal scholar counted just 23 cases between 1794 and 1860. And as recently as 1940, a total of only 1,513 malpractice cases were on the books. Another expert estimated that by 1955, only 1,936 medical malpractice cases had been ruled upon in state appeals courts; he also estimated, however, that about 100 times as many suits had initially been filed. (Most were settled out of court.)

Malpractice Insurance

Today, malpractice suits occur with great frequency, and juries often award enormous settlements to patients seeking payment for damages they claim to have suffered at the hands of a doctor or a hospital. A report prepared in 1977 by the Department of Health and Human Services found that the average amount of money juries awarded to patients who filed malpractice suits had soared 94% since 1970. The average award for temporary or insignificant injuries ran to about $7,500; patients who suffered permanent but not totally disabling injuries received an average of $150,000; the family of someone who had died from inadequate care usually was awarded about $57,600.

In order to ward off potential ruin, physicians pay steep sums for malpractice insurance. But this merely transfers the financial burden to insurance companies, which balk at the expense. Some have responded by sharply raising the cost of premiums (insurance fees). Others have stopped issuing policies altogether.

Yet the picture is not as bleak as it seems. Indeed, the statistics about medical malpractice cases can be read in different ways. Experts cited in Tom Christoffel's *Health and the Law* observe that although a few major malpractice suits have been highly publicized, the actual number of incidents of malpractice is relatively low, the number of lawsuits is small, and the number of cases that eventually go to trial is even fewer. When they do, juries rule in favor of the doctor 75% of the time. Most doctors go through their entire careers without ever being sued; of the rest, few are rarely sued more than once. And most hospitals, big or small, go through an entire year without being sued.

Nonetheless, the fear of suit affects almost every aspect of the medical profession. It can determine the decisions doctors and hospitals make about the type of medical treatment they give, the availability of certain health-care services, and the kind of relationship doctors have with their patients. The medical malpractice "crisis" also has had a major impact on the way such cases are handled in the legal system. Between 1975 and 1976, all 50 states passed laws dealing with one aspect or another of medical malpractice, changing the procedures for resolving these disputes.

For about 10 years, the problems with malpractice lawsuits seemed to stabilize, but by 1985 the doctor-versus-lawyer battle began heating up again. The number of lawsuits filed, the amount of average damages awarded, and the rates charged by the insurance companies began to skyrocket. In 1976, about 3 doctors out of 100 were subjected to malpractice claims; by 1986, the figure was up to 20 doctors out of 100; between 1974 and 1985, the average medical malpractice award rose from $166,165 to $1,179,095, and insurance fees rose between 400% and 600% during the same 10-year period. As of the mid-1980s, permission rates ranged from about $2,000 a year for a family doctor in a rural area to $100,000 a year for some specialists. The average insurance premium in 1985 reached $16,000 a year.

Skyrocketing insurance rates have especially hurt obstetricians, who treat infertility and deal with normal pregnancies and the delivery of babies; gynecologists, who treat women's reproductive organs and diseases; orthopedists, who treat skeletal deformities; and neurosurgeons, who operate on the brain and nervous system. All these are delicate, risky medical areas, and mistakes can be grave.

But as an obstetrician in Washington, D.C., complained to *Newsweek* magazine, a medical procedure that fails does not always mean the doctor who performed it was negligent, careless, or remiss. "Malpractice used to mean negligence or error. Now it simply means a bad result," the doctor said. Some doctors say society—and its legal system—demand the impossible. Doctors cannot be expected to succeed every time. Others argue that the medical establishment itself encourages patients to have high expectations and that it refuses to discipline bad doctors.

Torts

The law defines malpractice or negligence as the failure of a health-care provider to treat a patient with the care expected of the average, qualified practitioner. Patients are not necessarily entitled to recover from their ailment, but they are entitled to a careful diagnosis and a well-considered plan of treatment. They cannot expect to be awarded money simply because a treatment fails.

Malpractice lawsuits come under the legal category known as tort cases. A tort (from the Latin word for "twisted") is an injury someone has suffered because of another person's action—or inaction. People who allege that a tort, or injury, has been commited against them usually seek money as compensation.

In order for a patient or a patient's family to prove negligence, four tests must be met. They are duty, breach, causation, and damages.

The person filing suit—the plaintiff—must first show that the doctor, hospital, or health-care provider owed the patient a duty; namely, to provide medical care that meets the reasonable standard for all such treatment under equivalent circumstances. If the plaintiff establishes the duty owed by the doctor, he or she next must show that the doctor, hospital, or health-care provider breached, or failed to live up to, this obligation. Did the defendant do something or fail to do something and thus not provide the kind of medical care the patient could reasonably expect?

Third, the plaintiff must prove that the defendant's breach directly caused real harm to the patient. No matter how negligent a health-care provider may have been, damages will not be awarded unless the plaintiff can show a direct cause-and-effect relationship between the negligent act and the injury for which damages are being sought. Moreover, the harm must be measurable; disappointment and inconvenience will not suffice.

Even after all these tests have been met, the plaintiff cannot win the case unless damages (loss or harm resulting from injury to person, property, or reputation), the fourth test for malpractice, can be proved. This last hurdle is the most difficult. How can a judge or a jury—who lack medical expertise—decide what is the "reasonable standard of care" a patient can expect to receive?

The Locality Rule

For many years, judges often ruled that the standard a physician had to meet should be measured on the basis of the care offered by the doctors in the same or similar communities. This "locality rule" meant that a doctor in, say, a small town could not be expected to meet the standard of treatment provided by a better-trained, more experienced doctor in a big city. Thus, plaintiffs had to find a local doctor to testify against the defendant. This was no easy feat. Physicians dislike questioning the judgment of fellow professionals. As a result, doctors were sometimes accused of participating in a "conspiracy of silence" to protect one another from lawsuits.

Gradually, as general medical education improved and advanced procedures became widely publicized, the locality rule faded from use. In 1968, a Massachusetts court abolished it altogether. Most states now agree that health care should meet the same standards throughout the country, although a few state courts have stuck to the locality rule. In 1976, for example, experts from New York were not allowed to testify in a Louisiana malpractice case. And in 1977, doctors from Minnesota were not allowed to testify about the standard of practice in a Michigan community. Medical specialists were never protected by the locality rule. They were presumed to measure up to a national standard of education and treatment established by regulatory bodies and professional organizations.

As the locality rule became outmoded, plaintiffs fared more favorably in malpractice suits. They also profited from the more frequent use and acceptance of two other common law principles: *res ipsa loquitur*, a Latin phrase that means "the thing speaks for itself," and the concept of informed consent (see Chapter 4).

Res Ipsa Loquitur

The concept of res ipsa loquitur was first used successfully in a malpractice case in 1912 in which a surgeon was found guilty of negligence because he accidentally left a piece of gauze inside a patient. Thereafter, a number of cases were decided in favor of plaintiffs who were injured by the use of general anesthetic; common sense dictated that accidents could happen only if someone—either a doctor or a nurse—was negligent.

In order for a judge to decide whether a malpractice case can be tried on the basis of res ipsa loquitur, the plaintiff must demonstrate that the defendant was negligent, that the defendant had direct control over the apparent cause of that injury, and that the patient did nothing that contributed to the injury.

Defense lawyers argue that res ipsa loquitur should be applied only in cases in which it seems obvious that the doctor, hospital, or health-care provider made a mistake. The lawyers for plaintiffs counter that the rule should be applied often, in order to over-come, according to *Law for the Medical Office*, "the notorious unwillingness of members of the medical profession to testify against one another."

An Array of Defendants

Malpractice suits do not exclusively target doctors. All health-care professionals and facilities are expected to meet the accepted standards for qualified professionals.

Health-care providers are responsible not only for their own negligent actions but also, in some instances, for the negligence of their subordinates and employees. The legal terms often used to describe this principle are either the doctrine of *respondeat superior* ("let the master answer"); or vicarious (substitute) lia-bility, or the "captain of the ship doctrine." This does not mean the offending employee gets off scot-free. The law holds everyone liable for his or her own negligence.

A hospital hires staff nurses, dietitians, interns, residents, or-derlies, janitors, and so on, and therefore is normally liable for any negligent act those employees commit during the "course and scope" of their duties. "Course" of employment means during a regular business day; the "scope" of their employment refers to the extent of the responsibility given to the employee by his or her employer. Doctors who are in private practice but who have staff privileges at a hospital often give hospital employees instructions on how to treat the doctors' patients. If a hospital nurse, intern, or resident fails to carry out those instructions properly and, as a result, the patient suffers, the hospital, as employer, is liable for damages, not the doctor who gave the instructions.

THE MAIN CRIME: NEGLIGENCE

Negligence is not easy to prove, but defending oneself against a charge of negligence is not easy, either. It can cost doctors a lot of money and time and can harm their reputation—even if they are cleared of all charges.

Some Defenses

The most common response to an accusation of malpractice is a "denial defense": The defendant denies any negligence and therefore denies that he or she is to blame for the plaintiff's alleged injury. In most cases, however, the health-care provider will counter the evidence with his or her own testimony or with that of expert witnesses.

If the defendant opts for an "affirmative defense," the attorney can give the judge or jury new factual information in an effort to show that the plaintiff's condition has a cause other than the doctor's negligence. The physician may also contend that the injury is at least partly the patient's fault. In some states, evidence of a patient's "contributory negligence" bars him or her from winning any damages. In other states, the "doctrine of comparative negligence" is used: If the doctor can show that, for example, 10% to 20% of a patient's injury stems from his or her own negligence, the award is reduced by that percentage.

Another affirmative defense is called the "assumption of risk" defense. This means the patient's condition is attributable to the risky nature of the medical procedure the doctor used and that from the outset the patient knew the danger involved. Similarly, some defendants claim that circumstances beyond their control—usually a life-threatening emergency—caused the injury, not the treatment, which met the expected standards.

Negligence Laws

Attorneys who represent doctors sometimes use technical legal arguments to seek dismissal of lawsuits against their clients. One such argument is the "statute of limitations." This refers to the time period after which a patient cannot sue for malpractice. Statutes vary greatly from state to state, not only in length (often three or four years after the alleged negligence occurred), but also in the means of deciding when the clock starts ticking.

Many states say it begins ticking the day after the alleged negligence occurred. If the patient did not discover any wrongdoing until after the statute of limitations expired, he or she is out of luck. Several states have recently adopted a different policy, the so-called discovery rule. It holds that the time period in which a negligence suit can be filed does not begin until the patient actually discovers or should have discovered the injury, no matter when it occurred. This statute recognizes that most patients do not discover negligence until an ailment causes them to visit another doctor, who points out the error made by the first physician.

SPECIAL CIRCUMSTANCES

Most states also recognize special circumstances, such as a deliberate effort on the part of the doctor to hide the true nature of the patient's condition. An unusual example occurred in 1988 when the Maryland Court of Appeals, the state's highest court, ruled that a woman had the right to sue her former doctor for the "wrongful death" of her husband 13 years after he died and 10 years after the statutory limitation for filing suit had expired because there was evidence that the doctor defrauded the woman and her husband by repeatedly and "recklessly" assuring them that the man was receiving the proper treatment for his cancer when, in fact, he was not.

Another special circumstance applies when state prosecutors uncover frauds committed by health-care providers who serve Medicaid patients. In addition, doctors who are negligent in their treatment of patients can also be brought to trial on criminal charges—for instance if they perform surgery on a patient without obtaining his or her consent or if they sexually assault a patient who has been put to sleep with an anesthetic.

Manufacturers

Manufacturers of defective medical products or nonmedical goods that contribute to or cause illnesses also can be sued for damages. For example, in recent years the families of longtime smokers who died of lung cancer have filed a number of lawsuits against the tobacco companies that made the cigarettes. In 1988,

An attorney for the Liggett Group Inc., a cigarette manufacturer, leaves court after a jury awarded $400,000 in damages to Antonio Cipollone in 1988. Cipollone's wife, who had smoked cigarettes manufactured by Liggett for many years, died of lung cancer in 1984.

a New Jersey jury awarded $400,000 to Antonio Cipollone, whose wife, Rose, died of cancer in 1984 after having smoked for years the Chesterfield and L & M cigarettes manufactured by the Liggett Group Inc. In the first court decision of its kind, the jury decided that Liggett failed to warn Rose Cipollone adequately about the dangers of smoking. But it also found that she was 80% responsible for her conduct because she continued to smoke after learning of research linking smoking and cancer.

Later in 1988, a federal jury in St. Paul, Minnesota, awarded Esther Kociemba, 30, nearly $9 million in damages after ruling that G.D. Searle & Co. made intentional misstatements about its Copper-7 birth control device, one of the most widely used types of IUDs (intrauterine devices) in the country. The jury found that the device led to Kociemba's permanent inability to have children. Another medical appliance firm, A.H. Robins Company, which made the Dalkon Shield, another defective birth control device, has agreed to pay a total of at least $100 million to about 197,000 women who claimed the product harmed them. And in 1988, the U.S. Supreme Court let stand an $11.5 million damages award in another such product liability case, in which Playtex,

Inc. was found to be responsible for the 1983 death of Betty O'Gilvie, a Kansas woman who died of toxic shock syndrome, an illness caused, in this case, by the company's tampons.

CHANGING THE LAWS

As the pendulum has swung toward plaintiffs in malpractice suits, many doctors have adopted the practice of "defensive medicine." They often order more medical tests and procedures than are strictly necessary as a precaution against charges that they carelessly overlooked something that later harmed a patient. According to a survey by the American Medical Association reported in 1985, 27% of all doctors questioned said they had prescribed additional treatments, and 40% said they ordered additional medical tests for this reason. It is estimated that defensive medicine adds from $15 billion to $40 billion to the nation's health-care costs. Like rising insurance premiums, these extra defensive-medicine costs are ultimately borne by patients. "The doctor may be writing the checks, but society is paying the bill," an AMA official admitted in 1985.

The AMA has succeeded in persuading some state legislatures to change their malpractice laws. About half of the states have passed laws attempting to limit the circumstances under which malpractice suits can be filed or the amount of money plaintiffs can be awarded. In particular, the physicians want a cap placed on the damages a patient can win because of "pain and suffering or mental anguish," conditions that are hard to gauge in dollar value. How much mental anguish is there in losing a leg, and what is a fair amount of compensation for it? In 1975, California passed the first comprehensive law imposing limits on "pain and suffering" awards. As of 1989, a dozen more states had enacted such laws, despite opposition from the American Bar Association, the nation's largest lawyers' group.

Other AMA recommendations have also met with some success, although they still remain controversial. The change opposed most strenuously by lawyers involves the "contingency fee" that lawyers receive in malpractice cases; often it amounts to one-third of the settlement. Doctors argue that linking the lawyer's fee to the amount of money the plaintiff gets encourages attorneys to push for higher and higher damages; the lawyers contend that without contingency fees, only wealthy people would be able to file malpractice lawsuits.

California's 1975 law allows attorneys to keep as much as 40% of a settlement or judgment involving $50,000 or less, but the share of the damages that the lawyer can take as a fee then gradually declines to no more than 10% of an award over $200,000. Other states, including Wisconsin, Louisiana, Illinois, and Maryland, have created special panels of medical professionals to review alleged malpractice suits before they go to trial in order to determine if there is any merit to the charges. Some state laws also mandate pretrial arbitration, or mediation by a third party, of malpractice claims.

DISCIPLINING DOCTORS

On one issue the ABA and the AMA have found common ground: Incompetent doctors must be disciplined more harshly. In 1986, the federal government found that "strikingly few" doctors of questionable abilities (as determined by peer review groups) are kept from practicing. Of the country's 400,000 licensed physicians, between 20,000 and 45,000 "are likely candidates for some level of discipline," according to the report by the HHS inspector general. That figure is based on statistics regarding the level of alcoholism, drug addiction, mental illness, and other problems that afflict the whole population and, thus, probably affect doctors as well.

Yet, according to a study done by Public Citizen, a group created by consumer advocate Ralph Nader, only 563 doctors out of the nation's 400,000 physicians were disciplined by state review boards in 1983. In 1984, the medical licensing boards in the 50 states and the District of Columbia revoked the licenses of only 255 doctors, or 1 out of every 1,761 practicing physicians.

The HHS report urged new local, state, and national laws that would toughen disciplinary procedures, including methods for compelling cooperation from the various agencies responsible for reviewing doctors. Traditionally, state licensing boards often did not report the disciplining of a doctor to other states. As a result, doctors whose license had been revoked in one state simply moved to another state and obtained a new license to practice there. In 1984, the Federation of State Medical Boards began to computerize its nationwide list of the disciplinary actions taken against doctors. And, under the federal Health Care Quality Act, passed in 1986, HHS has been compiling a nationwide data bank listing disciplinary actions taken against specific physicians, dentists, nurses, therapists, and other licensed health-care professionals. The system was scheduled to be operational by 1989. Its information will be given to licensing boards, hospitals, and other medical groups, but not to the public.

Policing Themselves

About two-thirds of the states in the union have passed impaired-physician or "sick-doctor" laws since the late 1970s. These give state medical boards freedom to require a mental or physical examination for doctors whose abilities are believed to have been harmed by drugs or liquor. In addition, at least 11 states have passed "snitch" laws requiring physicians to report their incompetent colleagues to the state licensing board. These laws protect the reporting doctor from being sued by the accused physician, and in some states these laws have proved effective. In Arizona, for example, reports about incompetent doctors increased fourfold after that state's snitch law was passed.

State Medical Societies

Every state has a medical society—a professional organization of doctors. Most have created impaired-physicians committees that address the problems of alcoholic or drug-addicted doctors but keep the proceedings secret, even in states that require the medical societies to report all disciplinary actions.

The societies keep quiet partly because they fear being sued by the doctor they have disciplined and partly because they want to stand by their impaired colleague, whose addiction may worsen if he loses the right to practice. An official in New York's Office of Professional Misconduct has expressed frustration over this apparent reluctance on the part of doctors to clean their own house. "We want some guarantee that if a doctor is . . . a drunk or a drug addict, he won't be practicing medicine, but [the medical societies] often state that if the doctor can't work, it's bad for his self-esteem and he won't recover," she told the *New York Times*. "I don't mean to be cynical about this," the medical discipline official said, "but we are not primarily concerned with the doctor's self-esteem."

●　　　　●　　　　●　　　　●

CHAPTER 7

. . . .

ON THE EDGE
OF THE FUTURE

DNA pioneers James Watson (center) and Francis Crick (left, fore-ground).

"O brave new world,
That has such people in't!"

—William Shakespeare,
The Tempest

The most startling scientific advance of recent times was made in 1953, when researchers Francis Crick and James Watson uncovered the structure of DNA, the basic genetic building block of life. That breakthrough revolutionized the science of genetics. Doctors can now take a person's blood sample, extract genes from the blood cells, and examine or "screen" the genes in order to find evidence of diseases or physical defects that might afflict the person's children. This is an invaluable tool because genetic diseases cause immense human suffering, particularly for the newborn and the young.

HIGH-TECH SCREENING

Genetic defects are the second leading cause of death among children between the ages of 1 and 4 and are the third leading cause of death for 15 to 19 year olds. Twenty-five to 30% of all patients under 18 admitted to acute-care hospitals suffer from genetic ailments; and 20% to 25% of the mentally retarded people placed in institutions have other genetically caused illnesses. Parents and physicians can prepare for these difficulties through several sophisticated medical procedures. One of them, amniocentesis, tests cells in the fluid surrounding a fetus. Another, ultrasonography, uses sound waves to project an image of the fetus. Both procedures enable doctors to determine whether a fetus, if it becomes fully developed and is born, will have physical problems.

The Legal Consequences

As so often happens when science makes such significant advances, legislatures and the courts have struggled to respond with appropriate laws. For example, in the 1960s, almost every state passed laws requiring genetic screening tests for phenylketonuria (PKU), a serious genetic disease that can lead to severe mental retardation. In the 1970s, 17 states passed laws encouraging or requiring genetic screening for sickle-cell anemia, a genetically linked blood disease. More recently, states have been creating voluntary genetic-screening programs to uncover other illnesses.

These tests have placed new legal burdens on doctors, who now have a legal obligation to provide genetic counseling to patients who are thinking of having children or are already preg-

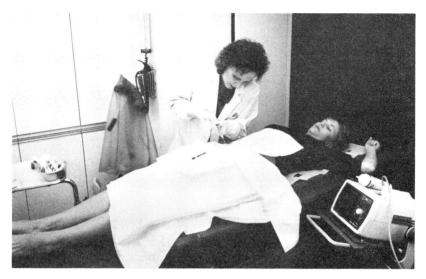

A pregnant woman undergoes an amniocentesis, in which the fluid in the uterus is examined for evidence of genetic defects. This is one of a series of technological procedures used to determine whether a fetus is healthy.

nant. And, not surprisingly, lawsuits have been filed by patients convinced that their doctors have failed to fulfill the obligation of thorough genetic screening.

Genetics and Cures

The science of genetics is not limited to predicting illnesses. Since 1973, when scientists first split the DNA molecule and developed the ability to combine, or recombine, pieces of DNA from different sources, efforts have been made to apply genetics to preventing or curing illnesses. Genetic engineering seemed to promise spectacular benefits in medicine, agriculture, and pollution control, but it also caused great concern about the dangers of unpredictable, man-made organisms escaping from laboratories; of terrorists using DNA research to create terrible biological-warfare weapons; of scientists trying to create new forms of life, "playing God."

In an unprecedented move, scientists voluntarily agreed to stop recombinant DNA research pending the results of a 1975 conference that addressed these issues. The conference urged the adoption of strict federal guidelines for DNA research, and scientists resumed their investigations. Since then, DNA research has developed rapidly and has brought medicine to the brink of genetic therapy. This research and the possible breakthroughs, however, remain extremely controversial.

MEDICINE, THE LAW, AND DEATH

Just as birth has been complicated by medical technology, so has death. The case of Karen Ann Quinlan (see Chapter 4) prompted many states to pass laws allowing people to forgo the extraordinary measures that would prolong life. But controversy engulfs living wills. What exactly did a person intend when he or she signed the document? In many states, the law clearly defines the

Scientists are developing increasingly sophisticated techniques and procedures that can treat illness, cure disease, and prolong life.

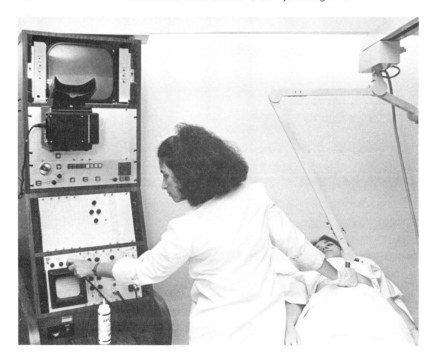

use of a mechanical respirator as an "extraordinary" treatment for permanently unconscious patients such as Karen Ann Quinlan. But is it also legal to unhook a person from the tubes and intravenous needles that supply him or her with food and water? As the head of a Baltimore hospital's intensive care unit recently told a reporter for the *Baltimore Sun*, "Technology allows us to keep bodies functioning. But you have to ask: Is this treatment rational?" There is no simple answer to that question—or to many other questions raised by the doctors and lawyers who wrestle with the perplexing issues of health care.

The legal system does the best it can, laboring under an avalanche of cases from which no type of doctor seems to be immune. The *Wall Street Journal* reported in 1988 that even veterinarians have not been immune to the malpractice crisis. Negligence claims against animal doctors are up, and so are damages awards against them. In the early 1980s, 1 out of 25 veterinarians faced a malpractice claim; by decade's end, 1 in 17 were hauled into court by grieving pet fanciers, farmers, and others, who charged them with negligence in their treatment of a cat, a dog, a cow, a horse, or some other animal. Malpractice insurance fees for horse doctors alone have gone up from about $2,000 a year to $1 million. The *Journal* also said that veterinarians were just the latest victims of "America's love affair with the legal brief."

This love seems to have become an obsession, as citizens increasingly rely on courts to settle disputes. As Tom Christoffel notes in *Health and the Law*, the United States has experienced "a widespread loss of trust in experts; a growing awareness of the effects of environmental and occupational hazards on health; a heightened interest in the public's right to information on oneself; mushrooming federal expenditures on health care, with a variety of regulatory strings attached; and a willingness of courts to deal with matters they had largely ignored in the past." The health-care industry is now the nation's largest employer; each day more than $1 billion is spent on it. "Sheer size and complexity in any industry will increase the role played by law and lawyers," Christoffel noted. "Certainly this is the case when the matters dealt with—health, illness and death—are very much both public and individual concerns."

Ultimately, however, both law and medicine have the same goal, one that may always elude their grasp. The matter has been summed up neatly by Dr. Oliver C. Schroeder, director of the law-medicine center at Case Western Reserve University in Cleveland: "Truth is pursued by law and medicine, not captured."

•   •   •   •

APPENDIX:
FOR MORE INFORMATION

The following is a list of organizations and associations that can provide further information on medicine and the law and on other related areas.

American Academy of Forensic
Sciences (AAFS)
225 South Academy Boulevard,
Suite 201
Colorado Springs, CO 80910
(303) 596-6006

American Academy of Hospital
Attorneys (AAHA)
American Hospital Association
840 North Lake Shore Drive
Chicago, IL 60611
(312) 280-6601

American Academy of Medical-
Legal Analysis (AAMLA)
522 Rossmore Drive
Las Vegas, NV 89110
(702) 385-6886

American Academy of Psychiatry
and the Law (AAPL)
1211 Cathedral Street
Baltimore, MD 21201
(301) 539-0379

American Association of Medical
Assistants
20 North Wacker Drive, Suite 1575
Chicago, IL 60606
(312) 899-1500

American Association of Medico-
Legal Consultants
Park Towne Place North
2200 Benjamin Franklin Parkway
Philadelphia, PA 19130
(215) 561-2121

American College of Legal Medicine
875 North Michigan Avenue
Suite 3342
Chicago, IL 60611
(312) 440-0080

American College of Obstetricians
and Gynecologists (ACOG)
P.O. Box 25
River Forest, IL 60305
(312) 383-1461

American Law Institute
4025 Chestnut Street
Philadelphia, PA 19104
(215) 243-1600

American Polygraph Association
(APA)
P.O. Box 8037
Chattanooga, TN 37411
(615) 892-3992

American Society of Law and
  Medicine, Inc.
520 Commonwealth Avenue
Suite 212
Boston, MA 02215
(617) 262-4990

American Tort Reform Association
  (ATRA)
1015 15th Street NW, Suite 802
Washington, DC 20005
(202) 347-7474

Association of Food and Drug
  Officials
P.O. Box 3425
York, PA 17402
(717) 757-2888

Canadian Association for Treatment
  of Offenders
2282 Clarke Drive
Abbotsford, British Columbia
V2S 3V3, Canada
(604) 853-9081

Concern For Dying (CFD)
250 West 57th Street
New York, NY 10107
(212) 246-6962

International Association of
  Coroners and Medical Examiners

2121 Adelbert Road
Cleveland, OH 44106
(216) 721-5610

International Center for Medicine
  and Law (ICML)
17 Battery Place, Suite 1223
New York, NY 10004
(212) 747-1756

National Forensic Center (NFC)
17 Temple Terrace
Lawrenceville, NJ 08648
(609) 883-0550

National Health Law Program
  (NHeLP)
2639 South LaCienega Blvd.
Los Angeles, CA 90034
(213) 204-6010

State Medicaid Directors
  Association (SMDA)
1125 15th Street NW
Washington, DC 20005
(202) 293-7550

Society for the Right To Die (SRD)
250 West 57th Street
New York, NY 10107
(212) 246-6973

FURTHER READING

Altman, Lawrence K. *Who Goes First? The Story of Self-Experimentation in Medicine.* New York: Random House, 1987.

Annas, George J., Leonard H. Glantz, and Barbara F. Katz. *The Rights of Doctors, Nurses, and Allied Health Professionals.* New York: Avon, 1981.

Chapman, Carleton B. *Physicians, Law and Ethics.* New York: New York University Press, 1984.

Childress, James F., and Ruth D. Gaare, eds. *BioLaw: A Legal Reporter on Medicine, Health Care, and Bioengineering.* Frederick, MD: University Publications of America, 1986.

Christoffel, Tom. *Health and the Law: A Handbook for Health Professionals.* New York: Avon, 1981.

Curran, William J., A. Louis McGarry, and Charles S. Petty. *Modern Legal Medicine, Psychiatry, and Forensic Science.* Philadelphia: F. A. Davis, 1980.

Dornette, William H. L., ed. *AIDS and the Law.* New York: Wiley, 1987.

Downing, A. B., and Barbara Smolen. *Voluntary Euthanasia: Experts Debate the Right to Die.* London: Peter Owen, 1986.

Eckstein, Harry. *The English Health Service: Its Origins, Structure, and Achievements.* Cambridge: Harvard University Press, 1958.

Fiscia, Salvatore F., et al. *A Sourcebook for Research in Law and Medicine.* Owings Mills, MD: National Health Publishing, 1985.

Foley, John P. *The Jefferson Cyclopedia.* New York: Funk & Wagnalls, 1900.

Gemmill, Paul F. *Britain's Search for Health: The First Decade of the National Health Service.* Philadelphia: University of Pennsylvania Press, 1960.

Gradwohl, R. B. H. *Gradwohl's Legal Medicine.* (3rd ed., ed. Francis E. Camps.) London: A. John Wright & Sons, 1976.

Gross, Stanley J. *Of Foxes and Hen Houses: Licensing and the Health Professions.* Westport, CT: Quorum Books, 1984.

Hershey, Nathan, and Robert D. Miller. *Human Experimentation and the Law.* Germantown, MD: Aspen, 1976.

Holbrook, Stewart H. *The Golden Age of Quackery.* New York: Macmillan, 1959.

Kapp, Marshal B., et al. *Legal and Ethical Aspects of Health Care for the Elderly.* Ann Arbor, MI: Health Administration Press, 1985.

Law for the Medical Office. Chicago: American Association of Medical Assistants, 1984.

Raffel, Marshall W. *Comparative Health Systems: Descriptive Analyses of 14 National Health Systems.* University Park, PA: Pennsylvania State University Press, 1984.

Shryock, Richard Harrison. *Medical Licensing in America, 1650–1965.* Baltimore: Johns Hopkins University Press, 1967.

Weir, Robert F., ed. *Ethical Issues in Death and Dying.* New York: Columbia University Press, 1986.

Winslade, William J., and Judith Wilson Ross. *The Insanity Plea: The Uses and Abuses of the Insanity Defense.* New York: Scribners, 1983.

GLOSSARY

acquit to find someone innocent of wrongdoing

action a lawsuit; the formal legal papers filed in court, demanding compensation from someone or correction of a situation

adversary process the legal procedure by which opposite sides in a dispute are given an equal chance to prove or disprove their claims

affirmative defense the presentation of evidence by the person against whom a lawsuit has been filed (the defendant), attempting to show that the matter that is in dispute was caused by something other than the defendant's actions or failure to act

AIDS acquired immune deficiency syndrome; an acquired defect in the immune system, thought to be caused by a virus (HIV) and spread by blood or sexual contact; leaves people vulnerable to certain, often fatal, infections and cancers

appeal the process by which a trial court's decision is reviewed by a higher court; the appeals court can either uphold or overturn the lower court's finding

arbitration the process by which a dispute is settled without going to court; both sides in the dispute agree to accept the decision of an impartial person or group who will hear evidence in a proceeding that is less formal than a trial

assault an intentional act that either threatens or causes harm to another person

autopsy a detailed examination of a dead body to determine the cause of death

battery the unlawful use of force upon a person without that person's consent; when a doctor gives more treatment to a patient than the patient has agreed to accept, a technical battery has occurred for which the patient can file suit to seek compensation

board of medical examiners a state agency that has the power to examine the qualifications of people who apply for medical licenses and to issue licenses to those who are qualified

burden of proof the responsibility of proving the charges in a legal case

captain-of-the-ship doctrine a legal rule under which the person "in charge" of a medical procedure—usually a doctor in an operating room—is held responsible for any mistakes by those working in the operating room

case a lawsuit, an action, a reason or cause for a legal dispute

certification a process by which persons involved in the practice of medicine demonstrate their skill by voluntarily taking part in evaluation programs designed to measure their knowledge and ability; those who meet the program's standards are awarded certificates

civil lawsuit a legal action that is filed to protect or obtain a private right or to correct something that has gone wrong

common law the law that is based on earlier court rulings or on custom rather than on statutes or regulations; it is sometimes called case law

consent a person's agreement to medical treatment; informed consent is consent based on the person's understanding of the possible positive or negative results of the treatment

contingency fee a fee arrangement under which a lawyer representing a person in a civil lawsuit receives a part of the money the client wins if the lawsuit is successful

contributory negligence often used by defendants, the argument that the person claiming an injury is partly responsible because of something that person did or failed to do, thus contributing to the problem

corporate negligence a legal theory that makes a hospital or business responsible for an injury caused by its employees or product

coroner a public official responsible for investigating any death that is not the result of natural causes

course and scope of employment a legal phrase that refers to those duties a person is hired for and expected to do while working for an employer

damages money awarded by a court or jury to someone who has suffered an injury or loss because of another's negligence or wrongdoing

defendant the person or institution against which a legal action is filed

due care the standard of care that a reasonable member of a profession would provide under the same or similar circumstances

due process of law the principle that fair procedures must be used whenever the freedom, property, and/or rights of a person are in question

emancipated minor a person under the legal age of majority (adulthood) who lives apart and independently from his or her parents and is completely self-supporting; emancipated minors are responsible for their own debts and may give consent for their own medical treatment

expert witness a person who testifies in court and has special knowledge about or training in the subject about which he or she is testifying

fraud an intentional effort to deceive someone else

good samaritan law a law in most states that gives legal immunity to people who provide first aid at the sites of accidents

incompetence the inability of a person to do something, either for mental, physical, or moral reasons

inquisitorial system a legal procedure common in France and other European countries in which witnesses in a legal dispute are called by the court, rather than by representatives of the defendant and plaintiff

liability a legal responsibility to do or not do something

license a permit given by a government agency that allows a person to do something—such as practice medicine—that is illegal without such permission

locality rule the use of the standards of a local community as a basis for judging the correctness of a person's conduct

malpractice the failure to meet a professional standard of medical care, resulting in harm to the patient

mature minor a teenager who is close to the age of majority, or legal adulthood, appears to fully understand the nature and the importance of a proposed medical treatment, and is thus capable of giving informed consent

Medicaid created by Congress in 1965; Medicaid is jointly operated by the federal government and the states and to provide health care for the poor

Medicare created by Congress in 1965, a national medical insurance program for the elderly and disabled; funded entirely by the federal government, it pays part, but not all, of the recipient's doctor and hospital bills

medical examiner a doctor who is a public official responsible for investigating sudden, unexplained, or apparently unnatural deaths; this investigation may include the performance of an autopsy

minor a person under the age of adulthood; in most states in the United States, a person becomes an adult in legal terms at the age of 18

moral turpitude dishonest or depraved behavior that reflects poorly on a person's character and may make him or her unqualified to practice a profession

National Health Service Great Britain's health insurance program, created in 1948, which provides free medical services to all citizens; it is the oldest operating national health system in the world

negligence failure to meet the standards of reasonable care under the same or similar conditions in which others meet that standard of care

opinion the explanation, often written, that is given by a court for its decision in a legal case

ordinance a law or rule passed by a local government body

plaintiff a person who, feeling wronged, files a lawsuit to seek correction of a problem or compensation for an injury

precedent a court decision that creates a legal principle by which later cases are decided

res ipsa loquitur a Latin phrase meaning, "The thing speaks for itself"; a legal doctrine under which negligence is implied by evidence of something a person did directly or over which the person had direct control

respondeat superior the Latin phrase, "Let the master answer"; a legal doctrine that makes the employer responsible for the negligent acts of an employee

statute a law passed by the legislature and signed by the governor at the state level or by the president at the federal level

statute of limitations the extent of the time period in which someone can file a lawsuit or bring charges against another person; it varies from state to state and from one type of case to another, but generally, with regard to medical malpractice cases, it is two to three years

suit the legal papers and legal process by which one side in a dispute attempts to prove a violation of rights and seeks a remedy or the enforcement of a right

tort a wrong or injury against another person, or against that person's property, for which a remedy or money can be sought

trial the actual presentation of evidence in court as part of a lawsuit

will a legal document that describes how a person wishes his or her property to be disposed of after death; a living will is a legal document in which a person states what medical procedures should be performed or withheld in the event of a terminal illness and the person's inability to express his or her wishes

wrongful birth a lawsuit filed by the parents of a handicapped or deformed child, claiming that they would not have conceived the baby or allowed it to be born but for the negligence of the doctor who counselled them

wrongful death a lawsuit filed by a dead person's family or heirs, charging that the person's death was caused by the negligent acts of another person

INDEX

PICTURE CREDITS

Neil A. Grauer is a free-lance writer and former newspaper reporter v.ho spent 10 years covering legal affairs, business, politics, and feature stories. He is the author and illustrator of *Wits and Sages*, a book of profiles and caricatures of leading syndicated columnists, and *Drugs and the Law* in the Chelsea House ENCYCLOPEDIA OF PSYCHOACTIVE DRUGS. He is also the public affairs officer in the Consumer Protection Division of the Maryland Attorney General's Office.

Dale C. Garell, M.D., is medical director of California Children Services, Department of Health Services, County of Los Angeles. He is also associate dean for curriculum at the University of Southern California School of Medicine and clinical professor in the Department of Pediatrics & Family Medicine at the University of Southern California School of Medicine. From 1963 to 1974, he was medical director of the Division of Adolescent Medicine at Children's Hospital in Los Angeles. Dr. Garell has served as president of the Society for Adolescent Medicine, chairman of the youth committee of the American Academy of Pediatrics, and as a forum member of the White House Conference on Children (1970) and White House Conference on Youth (1971). He has also been a member of the editorial board of the *American Journal of Diseases of Children.*

C. Everett Koop, M.D., Sc.D., is Surgeon General, Deputy Assistant Secretary for Health, and Director of the Office of International Health of the U. S. Public Health Service. A pediatric surgeon with an international reputation, he was previously surgeon-in-chief of Children's Hospital of Philadelphia and professor of pediatric surgery and pediatrics at the University of Pennsylvania. Dr. Koop is the author of more than 175 articles and books on the practice of medicine. He has served as surgery editor of the *Journal of Clinical Pediatrics* and editor-in-chief of the *Journal of Pediatric Surgery.* Dr. Koop has received nine honorary degrees and numerous other awards, including the Denis Brown Gold Medal of the British Association of Pediatric Surgeons, the William E. Ladd Gold Medal of the American Academy of Pediatrics, and the Copernicus Medal of the Surgical Society of Poland. He is a Chevalier of the French Legion of Honor and a member of the Royal College of Surgeons, London.

DATE DUE